BRIGANDS
of the
MOON

RAY CUMMINGS

Brigands of the Moon

Ray Cummings

PO Box 2211
Fairfield, IA 52556
www.1stworldlibrary.com
First Edition

LCCN: 2006935357

Softcover ISBN: 1-4218-2502-3
Hardcover ISBN: 1-4218-2402-7
eBook ISBN: 1-4218-2602-X

1st World Library Literary Society

Giving Back to the World

"If you want to work on the core problem, it's early school literacy."

- James Barksdale, former CEO of Netscape

"No skill is more crucial to the future of a child, or to a democratic and prosperous society, than literacy."

- Los Angeles Times

Literacy... means far more than learning how to read and write... The aim is to transmit... knowledge and promote social participation."

- UNESCO

"Literacy is not a luxury, it is a right and a responsibility. If our world is to meet the challenges of the twenty-first century we must harness the energy and creativity of all our citizens."

- President Bill Clinton

"Parents should be encouraged to read to their children, and teachers should be equipped with all available techniques for teaching literacy, so the varying needs and capacities of individual kids can be taken into account."

- Hugh Mackay

I

Our ship, the space-flyer, *Planetara,* whose home port was Greater New York, carried mail and passenger traffic to and from both Venus and Mars. Of astronomical necessity, our flights were irregular. The spring of 2070, with both planets close to the Earth, we were making two complete round trips. We had just arrived in Greater New York, one May evening, from Grebhar, Venus Free State. With only five hours in port here, we were departing the same night at the zero hour for Ferrok-Shahn, capital of the Martian Union.

We were no sooner at the landing stage than I found a code flash summoning Dan Dean and me to Divisional Detective Headquarters. Dan "Snap" Dean was one of my closest friends. He was electron-radio operator of the *Planetara.* A small, wiry, red-headed chap, with a quick, ready laugh and the kind of wit that made everyone like him.

The summons to Detective-Colonel Halsey's office surprised us. Dean eyed me.

"You haven't been opening any treasure vaults, have you, Gregg?"

"He wants you, also," I retorted.

He laughed. "Well, he can roar at me like a traffic switch-man and my private life will remain my own."

We could not think why we should be wanted. It was the darkness of mid-evening when we left the *Planetara* for Halsey's office. It was not a long trip. We went on the upper monorail, descending into the subterranean city at Park Circle 30.

We had never been to Halsey's office before. Now we found it to be a gloomy, vaultlike place in one of the deepest corridors. The door lifted.

"Gregg Haljan and Daniel Dean."

The guard stood aside. "Come in."

I own that my heart was unduly thumping as we entered. The door dropped behind us. It was a small blue-lit apartment - a steel-lined room like a vault.

Colonel Halsey sat at his desk. And the big, heavy-set, florid Captain Carter - our commander on the *Planetara* - was here. That surprised us: we had not seen him leave the ship.

Halsey smiled at us gravely. Captain Carter spoke with an ominous calmness: "Sit down, lads."

We took the seats. There was an alarming solemnity about this. If I had been guilty of anything that I could think of, it would have been frightening. But Halsey's words reassured me.

"It's about the Grantline Moon Expedition. In spite of our secrecy, the news has gotten out. We want to know how. Can you tell us?"

Captain Carter's huge bulk - he was about as tall as I am - towered over us as we sat before Halsey's desk. "If you lads have told anyone - said anything - let *slip* the slightest hint about it...."

Snap smiled with relief; but he turned solemn at once. "I

haven't. Not a word!"

"Nor have I!" I declared.

The Grantline Moon Expedition! We had not thought of that as a reason for this summons. Johnny Grantline was a close friend of ours. He had organized an exploring expedition to the Moon. Uninhabited, with its bleak, forbidding, airless, waterless surface, the Moon - even though so close to the Earth - was seldom visited. No regular ship ever stopped there. A few exploring parties of recent years had come to grief.

But there was a persistent rumor that upon the Moon, mineral riches of fabulous wealth were awaiting discovery. The thing had already caused some interplanetary complications. The aggressive Martians would be only too glad to explore the Moon. But the United States of the World, which came into being in 2067, definitely warned them away. The Moon was Earth territory, we announced, and we would protect it as such.

There was, nevertheless, a realization by our government, that whatever riches might be upon the Moon should be seized at once and held by some reputable Earth Company. And when John Grantline applied, with his father's wealth and his own scientific record of attainment, the government was glad to grant him its writ.

The Grantline Expedition had started six months ago. The Martian government had acquiesced to our ultimatum, yet brigands have been known to be financed under cover of a government disavowal. And so our expedition was kept secret.

My words need give no offence to any Martian who comes upon them. I refer to the history of our Earth only. The Grantline Expedition was on the Moon now. No word had come from it. One could not flash helios even in code without letting all the universe know that explorers were on the Moon. And why they were there, anyone could easily guess.

And now Colonel Halsey was telling us that the news was abroad! Captain Carter eyed us closely; his flashing eyes under the white bushy brows would pry a secret from anyone.

"You're sure? A girl of Venus, perhaps, with her cursed, seductive lure! A chance word, with you lads befuddled by alcolite?"

We assured him that we had been careful. By the heavens, I know that I had been. Not a whisper, even to Snap, of the name Grantline in six months or more.

Captain Carter added abruptly, "We're insulated here, Halsey?"

"Yes. Talk as freely as you like. An eavesdropping ray will never get through to us."

They questioned us. They were satisfied at last that, though the secret had escaped, we had not given it away. Hearing it discussed, it occurred to me to wonder why Carter was concerned. I was not aware that he knew of Grantline's venture. I learned now the reason why the *Planetara*, upon each of her last voyages, had managed to pass fairly close to the Moon. It had been arranged with Grantline that if he wanted help or had any important message, he was to flash it locally to our passing ship. And this Snap knew, and had never mentioned it, even to me.

Halsey was saying, "Well, apparently we can't blame you: but the secret is out."

Snap and I regarded each other. What could anyone do? What would anyone dare do?

Captain Carter said abruptly, "Look here, lads, this is my chance now to talk plainly to you. Outside, anywhere outside these walls, an eavesdropping ray may be upon us. You know that? One may never even dare to whisper since that accursed ray was developed."

Snap opened his mouth to speak but decided against it. My heart was pounding.

Captain Carter went on: "I know I can trust you two more than anyone under me on the *Planetara.*"

"What do you mean by that?" I demanded. "What -"

He interrupted me. "Just what I said."

Halsey smiled grimly. "What he means, Haljan, is that things are not always what they seem these days. One cannot always tell a friend from an enemy. The *Planetara* is a public vessel. You have - how many is it, Carter? - thirty or forty passengers this trip tonight?"

"Thirty-eight," said Carter.

"There are thirty-eight people listed for the flight to Ferrok-Shahn tonight," Halsey said slowly. "And some may not be what they seem." He raised his thin dark hand. "We have information...." He paused. "I confess, we know almost nothing - hardly more than enough to alarm us."

Captain Carter interjected, "I want you and Dean to be on your guard. Once on the *Planetara* it is difficult for us to talk openly, but be watchful. I will arrange for us to be doubly armed."

Vague, perturbing words! Halsey said, "They tell me George Prince is listed for the voyage. I am suggesting, Haljan, that you keep your eye especially on him. Your duties on the *Planetara* leave you comparatively free, don't they?"

"Yes," I agreed. With the first and second officers on duty, and the Captain aboard, my routine was more or less that of an understudy.

I said, "George Prince? Who is he?"

"A mechanical engineer," said Halsey. "An underofficial of the Earth Federated Catalyst Corporation. But he associates with bad companions - particularly Martians."

I had never heard of this George Prince, though I was familiar with the Federated Catalyst Corporation, of course. A semi-government trust, which controlled virtually the entire Earth supply of radiactum, the catalyst mineral which was revolutionizing industry.

"He was in the Automotive Department," Carter put in. "You've heard of the Federated Radiactum Motor?"

We had, of course. It was a recent Earth discovery and invention. An engine of a new type, using radiactum as its fuel.

Snap demanded, "What in the stars has this got to do with Johnny Grantline?"

"Much," said Halsey quietly, "or perhaps nothing. But George Prince some years ago mixed in rather unethical transactions. We had him in custody once. He is known as unusually friendly with several Martians in Greater New York of bad reputation."

"Well?"

"What you don't know," Halsey said, "is that Grantline expects to find radiactum on the Moon."

We gasped.

"Exactly," said Halsey. "The ill-fated Ballon Expedition thought they had found it on the Moon, shortly after its merit was discovered. A new type of ore - a lode of it is there somewhere, without doubt."

He added vehemently, "Do you understand now why we should be suspicious of this George Prince? He has a criminal record. He has a thorough technical knowledge of radium ores. He associates with Martians of bad reputation. A large Martian company has recently developed a radiactum engine to compete with our Earth motor. There is very little radiactum available on Mars, and our government will not allow our own supply to be exported. What do you suppose that company on Mars would pay for a few tons of richly radioactive radiactum such as Grantline may have found on the Moon?"

"But," I objected, "That is a reputable Martian company. It's backed by the government of the Martian Union. The government of Mars would not dare -"

"Of course not!" Captain Carter exclaimed sardonically. "Not openly! But if Martian Brigands had a supply of radiactum I don't imagine where it came from would make much difference. The Martian company would buy it, and you know that as well as I do!"

Halsey added, "And George Prince, my agents inform me, seems to know that Grantline is on the Moon. Put it all together, lads. Little sparks show the hidden current.

"More than that: George Prince knows that we have arranged to have the *Planetara* stop at the Moon and bring back Grantline's ore.... This is your last voyage this year. You'll hear from Grantline this time, we're convinced. He'll probably give you the signal as you pass the Moon on your way out. Coming back, you'll stop at the Moon and transport whatever radiactum ore Grantline has ready. The Grantline Flyer is too small for ore transportation."

Halsey's voice turned grimly sarcastic. "Doesn't it seem queer that George Prince and a few of his Martian friends happen to be listed as passengers for this voyage?"

In the silence that followed, Snap and I regarded each other.

Halsey added abruptly:

"We had George Prince typed that time we arrested him four years ago. I'll show him to you."

He snapped open an alcove, and said to his waiting attendant "Flash on the type of George Prince."

Almost at once, the image glowed on the grids before us. He stood smiling sourly before us as he repeated the official formula:

"My name is George Prince. I was born in Greater New York twenty-five years ago."

I gazed at this televised image of George Prince. He stood somber in the black detention uniform, silhouetted sharply against the regulation backdrop of vivid scarlet. A dark, almost femininely handsome fellow, well below medium height - the rod checking him showed five foot four inches. Slim and slight. Long, wavy black hair, falling about his ears. A pale, clean-cut, really handsome face, almost beardless. I regarded it closely. A face that would have been beautiful without its masculine touch of heavy black brows and firmly set jaw. His voice as he spoke was low and soft; but at the end, with the concluding words, "I am innocent!" it flashed into strong masculinity. His eyes, shaded with long girlish black lashes, by chance met mine. "I am innocent." His curving sensuous lips drew down into a grim sneer....

Halsey snapped a button. He turned back to Snap and me as his attendant drew the curtain, hiding the black grid.

"Well, there he is. We have nothing tangible against him now. But I'll say this: he's a clever fellow, one to be afraid of. I would not blare it from the newscasters' stadium, but if he is hatching any plot, he has been too clever for my agents!"

We talked for another half-hour, and then Captain Carter

dismissed us. We left Halsey's office with Carter's final words ringing in our ears. "Whatever comes, lads, remember I trust you...."

* * * * *

Snap and I decided to walk part of the way back to the ship. It was barely more than a mile through this subterranean corridor to where we could get the vertical lift direct to the landing stage.

We started off on the lower level. Once outside the insulation of Halsey's office we did not dare talk of this thing. Not only electrical ears, but every possible eavesdropping device might be upon us. The corridor was two hundred feet or more below the ground level. At this hour of the night the business section was comparatively deserted. The stores and office arcades were all closed.

Our footfall echoed on the metal grids as we hurried along. I felt depressed and oppressed. As though prying eyes were upon me. We walked for a time in silence, each of us busy with memory of what had transpired at Halsey's office.

Suddenly Snap gripped me. "What's that?"

"Where?" I whispered.

We stopped at a corner. An entryway was here. Snap pulled me into it. I could feel him quivering with excitement.

"What is it?" I demanded in a whisper.

"We're being followed. Did you hear anything?"

"No!" Yet I thought now that I could hear something. Vague footfalls. A rustling. And a microscopic whine, as though some device were within range of us.

Snap was fumbling in his pocket. "Wait! I've got a pair of low-scale detectors."

He put the little grids against his ears. I could hear the sharp intake of his breath. Then he seized me, pulled me down to the metal floor of the entryway.

"Back, Gregg! Get back!" I could barely hear his whisper. We crouched as far back into the doorway as we could get. I was armed. My official permit for the carrying of the pencil heat ray allowed me always to have it with me. I drew it now. But there was nothing to shoot at. I felt Snap clamping the grids on my ears. And now I heard something! An intensification of the vague footsteps I had thought I heard before.

There was something following us! Something out in the corridor there now! The corridor was dim, but plainly visible, and as far as I could see it was empty. But there was something there. Something invisible! I could hear it moving. Creeping toward us. I pulled the grids off my ears.

Snap murmured, "You've got a local phone?"

"Yes. I'll get them to give us the street glare!"

I pressed the danger signal, giving our location to the operator. In a second we got the light. The street in all this neighborhood burst into a brilliant actinic glare. The thing menacing us was revealed! A figure in a black cloak, crouching thirty feet away across the corridor.

Snap was unarmed but he flung his hands out menacingly. The figure, which may perhaps not have been aware of our city safeguard, was taken wholly by surprise. A human figure, seven feet tall at the least, and therefore, I judged, a Martian man. The black cloak covered his head. He took a step toward us, hesitated, and then turned in confusion.

Snap's shrill voice was bringing help. The whine of a street guard's alarm whistle nearby sounded. The figure was making off! My pencil ray was in my hand and I pressed its switch. The tiny heat ray stabbed through the air, but I missed. The figure stumbled but did not fall. I saw a bare gray arm come from the cloak, flung up to maintain its balance. Or perhaps my pencil ray had seared his arm. The gray-skinned arm of a Martian.

Snap was shouting, "Give him another!" But the figure passed beyond the actinic glare and vanished.

We were detained in the turmoil of the corridor for ten minutes or more with official explanations. Then a message from Halsey released us. The Martian who had been following us in his invisible cloak was never caught.

We escaped from the crowd at last and made our way back to the *Planetara*, where the passengers were already assembling for the outward Martian voyage.

II

I stood on the turret balcony of the *Planetara* with Captain Carter and Dr. Frank, the ship surgeon, watching the arriving passengers. It was close to the zero hour; the level of the stage was a turmoil of confusion. The escalators, with the last of the freight aboard, were folded back. But the stage was jammed with incoming passenger luggage, the interplanetary customs and tax officials with their x-ray and zed-ray paraphernalia and the passengers themselves, lined up for the export inspection.

At this height, the city lights lay spread in a glare of blue and yellow beneath us. The individual local planes came dropping like birds to our stage. Thirty-eight passengers to Mars for this voyage, but that accursed desire of every friend and relative to speed the departing voyager brought a hundred or more extra people to crowd our girders and add to everybody's troubles.

Carter was too absorbed in his duties to stay with us long. But here in the turret Dr. Frank and I found ourselves at the moment with nothing much to do but watch.

Dr. Frank was a thin, dark, rather smallish man of fifty, trim in his blue and white uniform. I knew him well: we had made several flights together. An American - I fancy of Jewish ancestry. A likable man, and a skillful doctor and surgeon. He and I had always been good friends.

"Crowded," he said. "Johnson says thirty-eight. I hope they're experienced travelers. This pressure sickness is a rotten nuisance - keeps me dashing around all night assuring frightened women they're not going to die. Last voyage, coming out of the Venus atmosphere -"

He plunged into a lugubrious account of his troubles with space sick voyagers. But I was in no mood to listen to him. My gaze was down on the spider incline, up which, over the bend of the ship's sleek, silvery body, the passengers and their friends were coming in little groups. The upper deck was already jammed with them.

The *Planetara*, as flyers go, was not a large vessel. Cylindrical of body, forty feet maximum beam, and two hundred and seventy-five feet in length. The passenger superstructure - no more than a hundred feet long - was set amidships. A narrow deck, metallically enclosed, and with large bull's-eye windows, encircled the superstructure. Some of the cabins opened directly onto the deck. Others had doors to the interior corridors. There were half a dozen small but luxurious public rooms.

The rest of the vessel was given to freight storage and the mechanism and control compartments. Forward of the passenger structure the deck level continued under the cylindrical dome roof to the bow. The forward watch tower observatory was here, officers' cabins, Captain Carter's navigating rooms and Dr. Frank's office. Similarly, under the stern dome, was the stern watch tower and a series of power compartments.

Above the superstructure a confusion of spider bridges, ladders and balconies were laced like a metal network. The turret in which Dr. Frank and I now stood was perched here. Fifty feet away, like a bird's nest, Snap's instrument room stood clinging to the metal bridge. The dome roof, with the glassite windows rolled back now, rose in a mound peak to cover the highest middle portion of the vessel.

Below, in the main hull, blue lit metal corridors ran the entire length of the ship. Freight storage compartments; gravity control rooms; the air renewal system; heater and ventilators and pressure mechanisms - all were located there. And the kitchens, stewards' compartments, and the living quarters of the crew. We carried a crew of sixteen, this voyage, exclusive of the navigating officers, the purser, Snap Dean, and Dr. Frank.

The passengers coming aboard seemed a fair representation of what we usually had for the outward voyage to Ferrok-Shahn. Most were Earth people - and returning Martians. Dr. Frank pointed out one. A huge Martian in a grey cloak. A seven foot fellow.

"His name is *Set* Miko," Dr. Frank remarked. "Ever heard of him?"

"No," I said. "Should I?"

"Well -" The doctor suddenly checked himself, as though he were sorry he had spoken.

"I never heard of him," I repeated slowly.

An awkward silence fell between us.

There were a few Venus passengers. I saw one of them presently coming up the incline, and recognized her. A girl traveling alone. We had brought her from Grebhar, last voyage but one. I remembered her. An alluring sort of girl, as most of them are. Her name was Venza. She spoke English well. A singer and dancer who had been imported to Greater New York to fill some theatrical engagement. She'd made quite a hit on the Great White Way.

She came up the incline with the carrier ahead of her. Gazing up, she saw Dr. Frank and me at the turret window, smiled and waved her white arm in greeting.

Dr. Frank laughed. "By the gods of the airways, there's Alta

Venza! You saw that look, Gregg? That was for me, not you."

"Reasonable enough," I retorted. "But I doubt it - the Venza is nothing if not impartial."

I wondered what could be taking Venza now to Mars. I was glad to see her. She was diverting. Educated. Well traveled. Spoke English with a colloquial, theatrical manner more characteristic of Greater New York than of Venus. And for all her light banter, I would rather put my trust in her than any Venus girl I had ever met.

The hum of the departing siren was sounding. Friends and relatives of the passengers were crowding the exit incline. The deck was clearing. I had not seen George Prince come aboard. And then I thought I saw him down on the landing stage, just arrived from a private tube car. A small, slight figure. The customs men were around him. I could only see his head and shoulders. Pale, girlishly handsome face; long, black hair to the base of his neck. He was bare-headed, with the hood of his traveling cloak pushed back.

I stared, and I saw that Dr. Frank was also gazing down. But neither of us spoke.

Then I said upon impulse, "Suppose we go down to the deck, Doctor?"

He acquiesced. We descended to the lower room of the turret and clambered down the spider ladder to the upper deck level. The head of the arriving incline was near us. Preceded by two carriers who were littered with hand luggage, George Prince was coming up the incline. He was closer now. I recognized him from the type we had seen in Halsey's office.

And then, with a shock, I saw it was not so. This was a girl coming aboard. An arc light over the incline showed her clearly when she was half way up. A girl with her hood pushed back; her face framed in thick black hair. I saw now it was not a man's cut of hair; but long braids coiled up under the dangling hood.

Dr. Frank must have remarked my amazed expression. "Little beauty, isn't she?"

"Who is she?"

We were standing back against the wall of the superstructure. A passenger was near us - the Martian whom Dr. Frank had called Miko. He was loitering here, quite evidently watching this girl come aboard. But as I glanced at him, he looked away and casually sauntered off.

The girl came up and reached the deck. "I am in A22," she told the carrier. "My brother came aboard a couple of hours ago."

Dr. Frank answered my whisper. "That's Anita Prince."

She was passing quite close to us on the deck, following the carrier, when she stumbled and very nearly fell. I was nearest to her. I leaped forward and caught her as she nearly went down.

With my arm about her, I raised her up and set her upon her feet again. She had twisted her ankle. She balanced herself upon it. The pain of it eased up in a moment.

"I'm all right - thank you!"

In the dimness of the blue lit deck I met her eyes. I was holding her with my encircling arm. She was small and soft against me. Her face, framed in the thick, black hair, smiled up at me. Small, oval face - beautiful - yet firm of chin, and stamped with the mark of its own individuality. No empty-headed beauty, this.

"I'm all right, thank you very much -"

I became conscious that I had not released her. I felt her hands pushing at me. And then it seemed that for an instant she yielded and was clinging. And I met her startled upflung gaze. Eyes like a purple night with the sheen of misty starlight in them.

I heard myself murmuring, "I beg your pardon. Yes, of course!" I released her.

She thanked me again and followed the carriers along the deck. She was limping slightly.

An instant she had clung to me. A brief flash of something, from her eyes to mine - from mine back to hers. The poets write that love can be born of such a glance. The first meeting, across all the barriers of which love springs unsought, unbidden - defiant, sometimes. And the troubadours of old would sing: "A fleeting glance; a touch; two wildly beating hearts - and love was born."

I think, with Anita and me, it must have been like that.

I stood, gazing after her, unconscious of Dr. Frank, who was watching me with his quizzical smile. And presently, no more than a quarter beyond the zero hour, the *Planetara* got away. With the dome windows battened tightly, we lifted from the landing stage and soared over the glowing city. The phosphorescence of the electronic tubes was like a comet's tail behind us as we slid upward.

III

At six A.M., Earth Eastern time, which we were still carrying, Snap Dean and I were alone in his instrument room, perched in the network over the *Planetara's* deck. The bulge of the dome enclosed us; it rounded like a great observatory window some twenty feet above the ceiling of this little metal cubbyhole.

The *Planetara* was still in Earth's shadow. The firmament - black, interstellar space with its blazing white, red and yellow stars - lay spread around us. The Moon, with nearly all its disc illumined, hung, a great silver ball, over our bow quarter. Behind it, to one side, Mars floated like the red tip of a smoldering cigar in the blackness. The Earth, behind our stern, was dimly, redly visible - a giant sphere, etched with the configurations of its oceans and continents. Upon one limb a touch of sunlight hung on the mountain tops with a crescent red-yellow sheen.

And then we plunged from the cone shadow. The Sun with the leaping corona, burst through the blackness behind us. The Earth lighted into a huge, thin crescent with hooked cusps.

To Snap and me, the glories of the heavens were too familiar to be remarked. And upon this voyage particularly we were in no mood to consider them. I had been in the radio room several hours. When the *Planetara* started, and my few routine duties were over, I could think of nothing save Halsey's and Carter's admonition: "Be on your guard. And particularly -

watch George Prince."

I had not seen George Prince. But I had seen his sister, whom Carter and Halsey had not bothered to mention. My heart was still pounding with the memory.

Dr. Frank evidently was having little trouble with pressure sick passengers. The *Planetara's* equalizers were fairly efficient. Prowling through the silent metal lounges and passages, I went to the door of A22. It was on the deck level, in a tiny transverse passage just off the main lounging room. Its name-grid glowed with the letters: *Anita Prince.* I stood in my short white trousers and white silk shirt, like a cabin steward staring. Anita Prince! I had never heard the name until this night. But there was magic music in it now, as I murmured it.

She was here, doubtless asleep, behind this small metal door. It seemed as though that little oval grid were the gateway to a fairyland of my dreams.

I turned away. Thought of the Grantline Moon Expedition stabbed at me. George Prince - Anita's brother - he whom I had been warned to watch. This renegade - associate of dubious Martians, plotting God knows what.

I saw, upon the adjoining door, A20, *George Prince.* I listened. In the humming stillness of the ship's interior there was no sound from these cabins. A20 was without windows, I knew. But Anita's room had a window and a door which gave upon the deck. I went through the lounge, out its arch and walked the deck length. The deck door and window of A22 were closed and dark.

The deck was dim with white starlight from the side ports. Chairs were here but they were all empty. From the bow windows of the arching dome a flood of moonlight threw long, slanting shadows down the deck. At the corner where the superstructure ended, I thought I saw a figure lurking as though watching me. I went that way, but it vanished.

I turned the corner, went the width of the ship to the other side. There was no one in sight save the observer on his spider bridge, high in the bow network, and the second officer, on duty on the turret balcony almost directly over me.

As I stood and listened, I suddenly heard footsteps. From the direction of the bow a figure came. Purser Johnson.

He greeted me. "Cooling off, Gregg?"

"Yes," I said.

He passed me and went into the smoking room door nearby.

I stood a moment at one of the deck windows, gazing at the stars; and for no reason at all I realized I was tense. Johnson was a great one for his regular sleep - it was wholly unlike him to be roaming about the ship at such an hour. Had he been watching me? I told myself it was nonsense. I was suspicious of everyone, everything, this voyage.

I heard another step. Captain Carter appeared from his chart room which stood in the center of the narrowing open deck space near the bow. I joined him at once.

"Who was that?" he half whispered.

"Johnson."

"Oh, yes." He fumbled in his uniform; his gaze swept the moonlit deck. "Gregg - take this." He handed me a small metal box. I stuffed it at once into my shirt.

"An insulator," he added swiftly. "Snap is in his office. Take it to him, Gregg. Stay with him - you'll have a measure of security - and you can help him to make the photographs." He was barely whispering. "I won't be with you - no use making it look as though we were doing anything unusual. If your graphs show anything - or if Snap picks up any message - bring it to me." He added aloud, "Well, it will be cool enough presently, Gregg."

He sauntered away toward his chart room.

"By heavens, what a relief!" Snap murmured as the current went on. We had wired his cubby with the insulator; within its barrage we could at least talk with a degree of freedom.

"You've seen George Prince, Gregg?"

"No. He's assigned A20. But I saw his sister. Snap, no one ever mentioned -"

Snap had heard of her, but he hadn't known that she was listed for this voyage. "A real beauty, so I've heard. Accursed shame for a decent girl to have a brother like that."

I could agree with him there....

It was now six A.M. Snap had been busy all night with routine cosmos-radios from the Earth, following our departure. He had a pile of them beside him.

"Nothing queer looking?" I suggested.

"No. Not a thing."

We were at this time no more than sixty-five thousand miles from the Moon's surface. The *Planetara* presently would swing upon her direct course for Mars. There was nothing which could cause passenger comment in this close passing of the Moon; normally we used the satellite's attraction to give us additional starting speed.

It was now or never that a message would come from Grantline. He was supposed to be upon the Earthward side of the Moon. While Snap had rushed through with his routine, I searched the Moon's surface with our glass.

But there was nothing. Copernicus and Kepler lay in full sunlight. The heights of the lunar mountains, the depths of the barren, empty seas were etched black and white, clear and clean. Grim, forbidding desolation, this unchanging Moon. In romance, moonlight may shimmer and sparkle to light a lover's smile; but the reality of the Moon is cold and bleak. There was nothing to show my prying eyes where the intrepid Grantline might be.

"Nothing at all, Snap."

And Snap's instruments, attuned for an hour now to pick up the faintest signal, were motionless.

"If he has concentrated any appreciable amount of ore," said Snap. "We should get an impulse from its rays."

But our receiving shield was dark, untouched. Our mirror grid gave the magnified images; the spectro, with its wave length selection, pictured the mountain levels and slowly descended into the deepest seas.

There was nothing.

Yet in those Moon caverns - a million million recesses amid the crags of that tumbled, barren surface - the pin point of movement which might have been Grantline's expedition could so easily be hiding! Could he have the ore insulated, fearing its rays would betray its presence to hostile watchers?

Or might disaster have come to him? He might not be on this hemisphere of the Moon at all....

My imagination, sharpened by fancy of a lurking menace which seemed everywhere about the *Planetara* this voyage, ran rife with fears for Johnny Grantline. He had promised to communicate this voyage. It was now, or perhaps never.

Six-thirty came and passed. We were well beyond the Earth's

shadow now. The firmament blazed with its vivid glories; the Sun behind us was a ball of yellow-red leaping flames. The Earth hung, a huge, dull red half sphere.

We were within forty thousand miles of the Moon. A giant white ball - all of its disc visible to the naked eye. It poised over the bow, and presently, as the *Planetara* swung upon its course for Mars, it shifted sidewise. The light of it glared white and dazzling in our windows.

Snap, with his habitual red celluloid eyeshade shoved high on his forehead, worked over our instruments.

"Gregg!"

The receiving shield was glowing a trifle. Rays were bombarding it! It glowed, gleamed phosphorescent, and the audible recorder began sounding its tiny tinkling murmurs.

Gamma rays! Snap sprang to the dials. The direction and strength were soon obvious. A richly radioactive ore body was concentrated upon this hemisphere of the Moon! It was unmistakable.

"He's got it, Gregg! He's -"

The tiny grids began quivering. Snap exclaimed triumphantly, "Here he comes! By God, the message at last!"

Snap decoded it.

Success! Stop for ore on your return voyage. Will give you our location later. Success beyond wildest hopes.

Snap murmured, "That's all. He's got the ore!"

We were sitting in darkness, and abruptly I became aware that across our open window, where the insulation barrage was flung, the air was faintly hissing. An interference there! I saw a tiny swirl of purple sparks. Someone - some hostile ray from the deck beneath us, or from the spider bridge that led to our little room - someone out there was trying to pry in!

Snap impulsively reached for the absorbers to let in the outside light. But I checked him.

"Wait!" I cut off our barrage, opened our door and stepped to the narrow metal bridge.

"You stay there, Snap!" I whispered. Then I added aloud, "Well, Snap, I'm going to bed. Glad you've cleaned up that batch of work."

I banged the door upon him. The lacework of metal bridges seemed empty. I gazed up to the dome, and forward and aft. Twenty feet beneath me was the metal roof of the cabin superstructure. Below it, both sides of the deck showed. All patched with moonlight.

No one visible down there. I descended a ladder. The deck was empty. But in the silence something was moving! Footsteps moving away from me down the deck! I followed; and suddenly I was running. Chasing something I could hear, but could not see. It turned into the smoking room.

I burst in. And a real sound smothered the phantom. Johnson the purser was sitting here alone in the dimness. He was smoking. I noticed that his cigar held a long frail ash. It could not have been him I was chasing. He was sitting there quite calmly. A thick-necked, heavy fellow, easily out of breath. But he was breathing calmly now.

He sat up in amazement at my wild-eyed appearance, and the ash jarred from his cigar.

"Gregg! What in the devil -"

I tried to grin. "I'm on my way to bed - worked all night

helping Snap."

I went past him, out the door into the main corridor. It was the only way the invisible prowler could have gone. But I was too late now - I could hear nothing. I dashed forward into the main lounge. It was empty, dim and silent, a silence broken presently by a faint click, a stateroom door hastily closing. I swung and found myself in a tiny transverse passage. The twin doors of A20 and A22 were before me.

The invisible eavesdropper had gone into one of these rooms! I listened at each of the panels, but there was only silence within.

The interior of the ship was suddenly singing with the steward's siren - the call to awaken the passengers. It startled me. I moved swiftly away. But as the siren shut off, in the silence I heard a soft, musical voice:

"Wake up, Anita, I think that's the breakfast call."

And her answer, "All right, George."

IV

I did not appear at that morning meal. I was exhausted and drugged with lack of sleep. I had a moment with Snap to tell him what had occurred. Then I sought out Carter. He had his little chart room insulated. And we were cautious. I told him what Snap and I had learned: the rays from the Moon, proving that Grantline had concentrated a considerable ore body. I also told him of Grantline's message.

"We'll stop on the way back, as he directs, Gregg." He bent closer to me. "At Ferrok-Shahn I'm going to bring back a cordon of Interplanetary Police. The secret will be out, of course, when we stop at the Moon. We have no right, even now, to be flying this vessel as unguarded as it is."

He was very solemn. And he was grim when I told him of the invisible eavesdropper.

"You think he overheard Grantline's message? Who was it? You seem to feel it was George Prince?"

I told him I was convinced the prowler went into A20. When I mentioned the purser, who seemed to have been watching me earlier in the night, and again was sitting in the smoking room when the eavesdropper fled past, Carter looked startled.

"Johnson is all right, Gregg."

"Does he know anything about this Grantline affair?"

"No - no," said Carter hastily. "You haven't mentioned it, have you?"

"Of course I haven't. But why didn't Johnson hear that eavesdropper? And what was he doing there, anyway, at that hour of the morning?"

The Captain ignored my questions. "I'm going to have that Prince suite searched - we can't be too careful.... Go to bed, Gregg, you need rest."

I went to my cabin. It was located aft, on the stern deck, near the stern watch tower. A small metal room with a chair, a desk and a bunk. I made sure no one was in it. I sealed the lattice grill and the door, set the alarm trigger against any opening of them, and went to bed.

The siren for the midday meal awakened me. I had slept heavily. I felt refreshed.

I found the passengers already assembled at my table when I arrived in the dining salon. It was a low vaulted metal room with blue and yellow tube lights. At its sides the oval windows showed the deck, with its ports on the dome side, through which a vista of the starry firmament was visible. We were well on our course to Mars. The Moon had dwindled to a pin point of light beside the crescent Earth. And behind them our Sun blazed, visually the largest orb in the heavens. It was some sixty-eight million miles from the Earth to Mars. A flight, ordinarily, of some ten days.

There were five tables in the dining salon, each with eight seats. Snap and I had one of the tables. We sat at the ends, with the passengers on each of the sides.

Snap was in his seat when I arrived. He eyed me down the length of the table. In a gay mood, he introduced me to the three men already seated:

"This is our third officer, Gregg Haljan. Big, handsome fellow, isn't he? And as pleasant as he is good-looking. Gregg, this is Sero Ob Hahn."

I met the keen, somber gaze of a Venus man of middle age. A small, slim graceful man, with sleek black hair. His pointed face, accentuated by the pointed beard, was pallid. He wore a white and purple robe; upon his breast was a huge platinum ornament, a device like a star and cross entwined.

"I am happy to meet you, sir." His voice was soft and deep.

"Ob Hahn," I repeated. "I should have heard of you, no doubt, but -"

A smile plucked at his thin, gray lips. "That is an error of mine, not yours. My mission is that all the universe shall hear of me."

"He's preaching the religion of the Venus mystics," Snap explained.

"And this enlightened gentleman," said Ob Hahn ironically, nodding to the man, "has just termed it fetishism. The ignorance -"

"Oh, I say!" protested the man at Ob Hahn's side. "I mean, you seem to think I meant something offensive. And as a matter of fact -"

"We've an argument, Gregg," laughed Snap. "This is Sir Arthur Coniston, an English gentleman, lecturer and sky-trotter - that is, he will be a sky-trotter; he tells us he plans a number of voyages."

The tall Englishman, in his white linen suit, bowed acknowledgement. "My compliments, Mr. Haljan. I hope you have no strong religious convictions, else we will make your table here very miserable!"

The third passenger had evidently kept out of the argument. Snap introduced him as Rance Rankin. An American - a quiet, blond fellow of thirty-five or forty.

I ordered my breakfast and let the argument go on.

"Won't make me miserable," said Snap. "I love an argument. You said, Sir Arthur -"

"I mean to say, I think I said too much. Mr. Rankin, you are more diplomatic."

Rankin laughed. "I am a magician," he said to me. "A theatrical entertainer. I deal in tricks - how to fool an audience -" His keen, amused gaze was on Ob Hahn. "This gentleman from Venus and I have too much in common to argue."

"A nasty one!" the Englishman exclaimed. "By Jove! Really, Mr. Rankin, you're a bit too cruel!"

I could see we were doomed to have turbulent meals this voyage. I like to eat in quiet; arguing passengers always annoy me. There were still three seats vacant at our table; I wondered who would occupy them. I soon learned the answer - for one seat at least. Rankin said calmly:

"Where is the little Venus girl this meal?" His glance went to the empty seat at my right hand. "The Venza, isn't that her name? She and I are destined for the same theater in Ferrok-Shahn."

So Venza was to sit beside me. It was good news. Ten days of a religious argument three times a day would be intolerable. But the cheerful Venza would help.

"She never eats the midday meal," said Snap. "She's on the deck, having orange juice. I guess it's the old gag about diet, eh?"

My attention wandered about the salon. Most of the seats were occupied. At the Captain's table I saw the objects of my search: George Prince and his sister, one on each side of the Captain. I saw George Prince in the life now as a man who looked hardly twenty-five. He was at this moment evidently in a gay mood. His clean-cut, handsome profile, with its poetic dark curls, was turned toward me. There seemed little of the villain about him.

And I saw Anita Prince now as a dark-haired, black-eyed little beauty, in feature resembling her brother very strongly. She presently finished her meal. She rose, with him after her. She was dressed in Earth-fashion - white blouse and dark jacket, wide, knee-length trousers of gray, with a red sash her only touch of color. She went past me, flashed me a smile.

My heart was pounding. I answered her greeting, and met George Prince's casual gaze. He, too, smiled, as though to signify that his sister had told him of the service I had done her. Or was his smile an ironical memory of how he had eluded me this morning when I chased him?

I gazed after his small white-suited figure as he followed Anita from the salon. And thinking of her, I prayed that Carter and Halsey might be wrong. Whatever plotting against the Grantline Expedition might be going on, I hoped that George Prince was innocent of it. Yet I knew in my heart it was a futile hope. Prince had been the eavesdropper outside the radio room. I could not doubt it. But that his sister must be ignorant of what he was doing, I was sure.

My attention was brought suddenly back to the reality of our table. I heard Ob Hahn's silky voice. "We passed quite close to the Moon last night, Mr. Dean."

"Yes," said Snap. "We did, didn't we? Always do - it's a technical problem of the exigencies of interstellar navigation. Explain it to them, Gregg. You're an expert."

I waved it away with a laugh. There was a brief silence. I could not help noticing Sir Arthur Coniston's queer look, and I have never seen so keen a glance as Rance Rankin shot at me. Were all three people aware of Grantline's treasure on the Moon? It suddenly seemed so. I wished fervently at that instant that the ten days of this voyage were over. Captain Carter was right. Coming back we should have a cordon of Interplanetary Police aboard.

Sir Arthur broke the awkward silence. "Magnificent sight, the Moon, from so close - though I was too much afraid of pressure sickness to be up to see it."

I had nearly finished my hasty meal when another incident shocked me. The two other passengers at our table came in and took their seats. A Martian girl and man. The girl had the seat at my left, with the man beside her. All Martians are tall. The girl was about my own height. That is, six feet, two inches. The man was seven feet or more. Both wore the Martian outer robe. The girl flung hers back. Her limbs were encased in pseudomail. She looked, as all Martians like to look, a very warlike Amazon. But she was a pretty girl. She smiled at me with a keen-eyed, direct gaze.

"Mr. Dean said at breakfast that you were big and handsome. You are."

They were brother and sister, these Martians. Snap introduced them as *Set* Miko and *Setta* Moa - the Martian equivalent of Mr. and Miss.

This Miko was, from our Earth standards, a tremendous, brawny giant. Not spindly, like most Martians, this fellow, for all his seven feet in height was almost heavy set. He wore a plaited leather jerkin beneath his robe and knee pants of leather out of which his lower legs showed as gray, hairy pillars of strength. He had come into the salon with a swagger, his sword ornament clanking.

"A pleasant voyage so far," he said to me as he started his meal. His voice had the heavy, throaty rasp characteristic of the Martian. He spoke perfect English - both Martians and Venus people are by heritage extraordinary linguists. Miko and his sister Moa, had a touch of Martian accent, worn almost away by living for some years in Greater New York.

The shock to me came within a few minutes. Miko, absorbed in attacking his meal, inadvertently pushed back his robe to bare his forearm. An instant only, then it dropped to his wrist. But in that instant I had seen, upon the gray flesh, a thin sear turned red. A very recent burn - as though a pencil ray of heat had caught his arm.

My mind flung back. Only last night in the city corridor, Snap and I had been followed by a Martian. I had shot at him with a heat ray: I thought I had hit him on the arm. Was this the mysterious Martian who had followed us from Halsey's office?

V

Shortly after that midday meal I encountered Venza sitting on the starlit deck. I had been in the bow observatory; taken my routine castings of our position and worked them out. I was, I think, of the *Planetara's* officers the most expert handler of the mathematical calculators. The locating of our position and charting the trajectory of our course was, under ordinary circumstances, about all I had to do. And it took only a few minutes every twelve hours.

I had a moment with Carter in the isolation of his chart room.

"This voyage! Gregg, I'm getting like you - too fanciful. We've a normal group of passengers apparently, but I don't like the look of any of them. That Ob Hahn, at your table -"

"Snaky looking fellow," I commented. "He and the Englishman are great on arguments. Did you have Princes' cabin searched?"

My breath hung on his answer.

"Yes. Nothing unusual among his things. We searched both his room and his sister's."

I did not follow that up. Instead I told him about the burn on Miko's thick arm.

He stared. "I wish we were at Ferrok-Shahn. Gregg, tonight

when the passengers are asleep, come here to me. Snap will be here, and Dr. Frank. We can trust him."

"He knows about - about the Grantline treasure?"

"Yes. And so do Balch and Blackstone." Balch and Blackstone were our first and second officers.

"We'll all meet here, Gregg - say about the zero hour. We must take some precautions."

Then he dismissed me.

I found Venza seated alone in a starlit corner of the secluded deck. A porthole, with the black heavens and the blazing stars was before her. There was an empty seat nearby.

She greeted me with the Venus form of jocular, intimate greeting:

"Hola-lo, Gregg! Sit here with me. I have been wondering when you would come after me."

I sat down beside her. "Why are you going to Mars, Venza? I'm glad to see you."

"Many thanks. But I am glad to see you, Gregg. So handsome a man. Do you know, from Venus to Earth, and I have no doubt on all of Mars, no man will please me more."

"Glib tongue," I laughed. "Born to flatter the male - every girl of your world." And I added seriously, "You don't answer my question. What takes you to Mars?"

"Contract. By the stars, what else? Of course, a chance to make a voyage with you -"

"Don't be silly, Venza."

I enjoyed her. I gazed at her small, slim figure reclining in the deck chair. Her long, gray robe parted by design, I have no doubt, to display her shapely, satin-sheathed legs. Her black hair was coiled in a heavy knot at the back of her neck; her carmine lips were parted with a mocking, alluring smile. The exotic perfume of her enveloped me.

She glanced at me sidewise from beneath her sweeping black lashes.

"Be serious," I added.

"I am serious. Sober. Intoxicated by you, but sober."

I said, "What sort of a contract?"

"A theater in Ferrok-Shahn. Good money, Gregg. I'll be there a year." She sat up to face me. "There's a fellow here on the *Planetara*, Rance Rankin, he calls himself. At our table - a big, good-looking blond American. He says he is a magician. Ever hear of him?"

"That's what he told me. No, I never heard of him."

"Nor did I. And I thought I had heard of everyone of importance. He is listed for the same theater I am. Nice sort of fellow." She paused, then added, "If he's a professional entertainer, I'm a motor oiler."

It startled me. "Why do you say that?"

Instinctively my gaze swept the deck. An Earth woman and child and a small Venus man were in sight, but not within earshot.

"Why do you look so furtive?" she retorted. "Gregg, there's something strange about this voyage. I'm no fool, nor you, so you must know it as well as I do."

"Rance Rankin -" I prompted.

She leaned closer toward me. "He could fool you. But not me - I've known too many magicians." She grinned. "I challenged him to trick me. You should have seen him evading!"

"Do you know Ob Hahn?" I interrupted.

She shook her head. "Never heard of him. But he told me plenty at breakfast. By Satan, what a flow of words that devil driver can muster! He and the Englishman don't mesh very well, do they?"

She stared at me. I had not answered her grin; my mind was too busy with queer fancies. Halsey's words: "Things are not always what they seem -" Were these passengers masqueraders? Were they put here by George Prince? And then I thought of Miko the Martian, and the burn upon his arm.

"Come back, Gregg! Don't go wandering off like that!" She dropped her voice to a whisper. "I'll be serious. I want to know what in hell is going on aboard this ship. I'm a woman and I'm curious. You tell me."

"What do you mean?" I parried.

"I mean a lot of things. What we've just been talking about. And what was the excitement you were in just before breakfast this morning?"

"Excitement?"

"Gregg, you may trust me." For the first time she was wholly serious. Her gaze made sure no one was within hearing. She put her hand on my arm. I could barely hear her whisper: "I know they might have a ray upon us. I'll be careful."

"They?"

"Anyone. Something's going on. You know it. You are in it. I saw you this morning, Gregg. Wild-eyed, chasing a phantom -"

"You?"

"And I heard the phantom! A man's footsteps. A magnetic, deflecting, invisible cloak. You couldn't fool an audience with that, it's too commonplace. If Rance Rankin tried -"

I gripped her. "Don't ramble, Venza! You saw me?"

"Yes. My stateroom door was open. I was sitting with a cigarette. I saw the purser in the smoking room. He was visible from -"

"Wait! Venza, that prowler went through the smoking room!"

"I know he did. I could hear him."

"Did the purser hear him?"

"Of course. The purser looked up, followed the sound with his gaze. I thought that was queer. He never made a move. And then you came along and he acted innocent. Why? What's going on, that's what I want to know?"

I held my breath. "Venza, where did the prowler run to? Can you -"

She whispered calmly, "Into A20. I saw the door open and close. I even thought I could see his blurred outline." She added, "Why should George Prince be sneaking around with you after him? And the purser acting innocent? And who is this George Prince, anyway?"

The huge Martian, Miko, with his sister Moa came strolling along the deck. They nodded as they passed us.

I whispered, "I can't explain anything now. But you're right, Venza: there is something going on. Listen! Whatever you learn - whatever you encounter which looks unusual - will you tell me? I ... well, I do trust you. Really I do, but the whole thing isn't mine to tell."

The somber pools of her eyes were shining. "You are very lovable, Gregg. I won't question you." She was trembling with excitement.

"Whatever it is, I want to be in on it. Here's something I can tell you now. We've two high class gold leaf gamblers aboard. Do you know that?"

"Who are they?"

"Shac and Dud Ardley. Every detective in Greater New York knows them. They had a wonderful game with that Englishman, Sir Arthur, this morning. Stripped him of half a pound of eight-inch leaves - a neat little stack. A crooked game, of course. Those fellows are more nimble-fingered than Rance Rankin ever dared to be!"

I sat staring at her. She was a mine of information, this girl.

"And Gregg, I tried my charms on Shac and Dud. Nice men, but dumb. Whatever's going on, they're not in it. They wanted to know what kind of a ship this was. Why? Because Shac has a cute little eavesdropping microphone of his own. He had it working last night. He overheard George Prince and that giant Miko arguing about the Moon!"

I gasped, "Venza! Softer -"

Against all propriety of this public deck she pretended to drape herself upon me. Her hair smothered my face as her lips almost touched my ear.

"Something about treasure on the Moon. Shac couldn't

understand what. And they mentioned you. Then the purser joined them." Her whispered words tumbled over one another. "A hundred pounds of gold leaf - that's the purser's price. He's with them - whatever it is. He promised to do something or other for them."

She stopped. "Well?" I prompted.

"That's all. Shac's current was interrupted."

"Tell him to try it again, Venza! I'll talk with him. No! I'd better let him alone. Can you get him to keep his mouth shut?"

"I think he might do anything I told him. He's a man!"

"Find out what you can."

She drew away from me abruptly. "There's Anita and George Prince."

They came to the corner of the deck, but turned back. Venza caught my look. And understood it.

"You do love Anita Prince, Gregg?" Venza was smiling. "I wish you.... I wish some man handsome as you would gaze after me like that." She turned solemn. "You may be interested to know, she loves you. I could see it. I knew it when I mentioned you to her this morning."

"Me? Why we've hardly spoken!"

"Is it necessary? I never heard that it was."

I could not see Venza's face; she stood up suddenly. And when I rose beside her, she whispered, "We should not be seen talking so long. I'll find out what I can."

I stared after her slight robed figure as she turned into the lounge archway and vanished.

VI

Captain Carter was grim. "So they've bought him off, have they? Go bring him in here, Gregg. We'll have it out with him now."

Snap, Dr. Frank, Balch, our first officer, and I were in the Captain's chart room. It was four P.M. Earth time. We were sixteen hours upon our voyage.

I found Johnson in his office in the lounge. "Captain wants to see you. Close up."

He closed his window upon an American woman passenger who was demanding the details of Martian currency, and followed me forward. "What is it, Gregg?"

"I don't know."

Captain Carter banged the slide upon us. The chart room was insulated. The hum of the current was obvious. Johnson noticed it. He stared at the hostile faces of the surgeon and Balch. And he tried to bluster.

"What's this? Something wrong?"

Carter wasted no words. "We have information, Johnson, that there's some undercover plot aboard. I want to know what it is. Suppose you tell us."

The purser looked blank. "What do you mean? We've gamblers aboard, if that's -"

"To hell with that," growled Balch. "You had a secret interview with that Martian, *Set* Miko, and with George Prince!"

Johnson scowled from under his heavy brows, and then raised them in surprise. "Did I? You mean changing their money? I don't like your tone, Balch. I'm not your under-officer!"

"But you're under me!" roared the Captain. "By God, I'm master here!"

"Well, I'm not disputing that," said the purser mildly. "This fellow -"

"We're in no mood for argument," Dr. Frank cut in. "Clouding the issue...."

"I won't let it be clouded," the Captain exclaimed.

I had never seen Carter so choleric. He added:

"Johnson, you've been acting suspiciously. I don't give a damn whether I've proof of it or not. Did you or did you not meet George Prince and that Martian, last night?"

"No, I did not. And I don't mind telling you, Captain Carter, that your tone also is offensive!"

"Is it?" Carter seized him. They were both big men. Johnson's heavy face went purplish red.

"Take your hands - !" They were struggling. Carter's hands were fumbling at the purser's pockets. I leaped, flung an arm around Johnson's neck, pinning him.

"Easy there! We've got you, Johnson!"

Snap tried to help me. "Go on! Bang him on the head, Gregg. Now's your chance!"

We searched him. A heat ray cylinder - that was legitimate. But we found a small battery and eavesdropping device similar to the one Venza had mentioned that Shac the gambler was carrying.

"What are you doing with that?" the Captain demanded.

"None of your business! Is it criminal? Carter, I'll have the line officials dismiss you for this! Take your hands off me - all of you!"

"Look at this!" exclaimed Dr. Frank.

From Johnson's breast pocket the surgeon drew a folded document. It was a scale drawing of the *Planetara* interior corridors, the lower control rooms and mechanisms. It was always kept in Johnson's safe. And with it, another document: the ship's clearance papers - the secret code passwords for this voyage, to be used if we should be challenged by any Interplanetary Police ship.

Snap gasped, "My God, that was in my radio room strong box! I'm the only one on this vessel except the Captain who's entitled to know those passwords!"

Out of the silence, Balch demanded, "Well, what about it, Johnson?"

The purser was still defiant. "I won't answer your questions, Balch. At the proper time, I'll explain - Gregg Haljan, you're choking me!"

I eased up. But I shook him. "You'd better talk."

He was exasperatingly silent.

"Enough!" exploded Carter. "He can explain when we get to port. Meanwhile I'll put him where he'll do no more harm. Gregg, lock him in the cage."

We ignored his violent protestations. The cage - in the old days of sea vessels on Earth, they called it the brig - was the ship's jail. A steel-lined, windowless room located under the deck in the peak of the bow. I dragged the struggling Johnson there, with the amazed watcher looking down from the observatory window at our lunging starlit forms.

"Shut up, Johnson! If you know what's good for you -"

He was making a fearful commotion. Behind us, where the deck narrowed at the superstructure, half a dozen passengers were gazing in surprise.

"I'll have you thrown out of the service, Gregg Haljan!"

I shut him up finally. And flung him down the ladder into the cage and sealed the deck trap door upon him. I was headed back for the chart room when from the observatory came the lookout's voice:

"An asteroid, Haljan! Officer Blackstone wants you."

I hurried to the turret bridge. An asteroid was in sight. We had nearly attained our maximum speed now. An asteroid was approaching, so dangerously close that our trajectory would have to be altered. I heard Blackstone's signals ringing in the control rooms; and met Carter as he ran to the bridge with me.

"That scoundrel! We'll get more out of him, Gregg. By God, I'll put the chemicals on him - torture him - illegal or not!"

We had no time for further discussion. The asteroid was rapidly approaching. Already, under the glass, it was a magnificent sight. I had never seen this tiny world before – asteroids are not numerous between the Earth and Mars, or in toward Venus.

At a speed of nearly a hundred miles a second the asteroid swept into view. With the naked eye, at first it was a tiny speck of star-dust unnoticeable in the gem-strewn black velvet of space. A speck. Then a gleaming dot, silver white, with the light of our Sun upon it.

I stood with Carter and Blackstone on the turret bridge. It was obvious, that unless we altered our course, the asteroid would pass too close for safety. Already we were feeling its attraction; from the control rooms came the report that our trajectory was disturbed by this new mass so near.

"Better make your calculations now, Gregg," Blackstone urged.

I cast up the rough elements from the observational instruments in the turret. When I had us upon our new course, with the attractive and repulsive plates in the *Planetara's* hull set in their altered combinations, I went to the bridge again.

The asteroid hung over our bow quarter. No more than twenty or thirty thousand miles away. A giant ball now, filling all that quadrant of the heavens. The configurations of its mountains, its land and water areas, were plainly visible.

"Perfectly habitable," Blackstone said. "But I've searched all over the hemisphere with the glass. No sign of human life – certainly nothing civilized - nothing in the fashion of cities."

A fair little world, by the look of it. A tiny globe, come from the region beyond Neptune. We swept past the asteroid. The passengers were all gathered to view the passing little world. I saw, not far from me, Anita, standing with her brother; and the giant figure of Miko with them. Half an hour since this wandering little world had showed itself, it swiftly passed, began to dwindle behind us. A huge half moon. A thinner, smaller quadrant. A tiny crescent, like a silver barpin to adorn some lady's breast. And then it was a dot, a point of light indistinguishable among the myriad others hovering in this great black void.

The incident of the passing of the asteroid was over. I turned from the deck window. My heart leaped. The moment for which all day I had been subconsciously longing was at hand. Anita was sitting in a deck chair, momentarily alone. Her gaze was on me as I glanced her way, and she smiled an invitation for me to join her.

VII

"But, Miss Prince, why are you and your brother going to Ferrok-Shahn? His business -"

Even as I voiced it, I hated myself for such a question. So nimble in the humble mind that mingled with my rhapsodies of love, was my need for information of George Prince.

"Oh," she said. "This is pleasure, not business, for George." It seemed to me that a shadow crossed her face. But it was gone in an instant, and she smiled. "We have always wanted to travel. We are alone in the world, you know - our parents died when we were children."

I filled in her pause. "You will like Mars. So many interesting things to see."

She nodded. "Yes, I understand so. Our Earth is so much the same all over, cast all in one mould."

"But a hundred or more years ago, it was not, Miss Prince. I have read how the picturesque Orient, differing from ... well, Greater New York or London, for instance -"

"Transportation did that," she interrupted eagerly. "Made everything the same - the people all look alike ... dress alike."

We discussed it. She had an alert, eager mind, childlike with its curiosity, yet strangely matured. And her manner was naively earnest. Yet this was no clinging vine, this Anita Prince. There was a firmness, a hint of masculine strength in her chin and in her manner.

"If I were a man, what wonders I could achieve in this marvelous age!" Her sense of humor made her laugh at herself. "Easy for a girl to say that," she added.

"You have greater wonders to achieve, Miss Prince," I said impulsively.

"Yes? What are they?" She had a very frank and level gaze, devoid of coquetry.

My heart was pounding. "The wonders of the next generation. A little son, cast in your own gentle image -"

What madness, this clumsy, brash talk! I choked it off.

But she took no offense. The dark rose-petals of her cheeks were mantled deeper red, but she laughed.

"That is true." She turned abruptly serious. "I should not laugh. The wonders of the next generation - conquering humans marching on...." Her voice trailed away. My hand went to her arm. Strange tingling something which poets call love! It burned and surged through my trembling fingers into the flesh of her forearm.

The starlight glowed in her eyes. She seemed to be gazing, not at the silver-lit deck, but away into distant reaches of the future.

Our moment. Just a breathless moment given us as we sat there with my hand burning her arm, as though we both might be seeing ourselves joined in a new individual - a little son, cast in his mother's gentle image and with the strength of his father. Our moment, and then it was over. A step sounded. I sat back. The giant gray figure of Miko came past, his great cloak swaying, with his clanking sword ornament beneath it. His bullet head, with its close-clipped hair, was hatless. He gazed at us, swaggering past, and turned the deck corner.

Our moment was gone. Anita said conventionally, "It has been pleasant to talk with you, Mr. Haljan."

"But we'll have many more," I said. "Ten days -"

"You think we'll reach Ferrok-Shahn on schedule?"

"Yes. I think so.... As I was saying, Miss Prince, you'll enjoy Mars. A strange, aggressively forward-looking people."

An oppression seemed on her. She stirred in her chair.

"Yes they are," she said vaguely. "My brother and I know many Martians in Greater New York." She checked herself abruptly. Was she sorry she had said that? It seemed so.

Miko was coming back. He stopped this time. "Your brother would see you, Anita. He sent me to bring you to his room."

The glance he shot me had a touch of insolence. I stood up and he towered a head over me.

Anita said, "Oh yes. I'll come."

I bowed. "I will see you again, Miss Prince. I thank you for a pleasant half-hour."

The Martian led her away. Her little figure was like a child with a giant. It seemed, as they passed the length of the deck, with me staring after them, that he took her arm roughly. And that she shrank from him in fear.

And they did not go inside. As though to show me that he had merely taken her from me, he stopped at a distant deck window and stood talking to her. Once he picked her up as one would pick up a child to show it some distant object through the window.

Was Anita afraid of this Martian's wooing? Yet was held to him by some power he might have over her brother? The vagrant thought struck me.

VIII

The rest of that afternoon and evening were a blank confusion to me. Anita's words, the touch of my hand on her arm, that vast realm of what might be for us, like the glimpse of a magic land of happiness which I had seen in her eyes, and perhaps she had seen in mine - all this surged within me.

After wandering about the ship, I had a brief consultation with Captain Carter. He was genuinely apprehensive now. The *Planetara* carried only a half-dozen of the heat-ray projectors, no long range weapons, a few side arms, and some old-fashioned, practically antiquated weapons of explosives, plus hand projectors with the new Benson curve light.

The weapons were all in Carter's chart room, save the few we officers always carried. Carter was afraid, but of what, he was not sure. He had not thought that our plan to stop at the Moon could affect this outward voyage. He had thought that any danger would occur on the way back, and then the *Planetara* would have been adequately guarded and manned with police-soldiers.

But now we were practically defenseless. I had a moment with Venza, but she had nothing new to communicate. And for half an hour I chatted with George Prince. He seemed a gay, pleasant young man. I could almost have fancied I liked him. Or was it because he was Anita's brother? He told me how he looked forward to traveling with her on Mars. No, he had never been there before, he said.

He had a measure of Anita's earnest naive personality. Or was he a very clever scoundrel, with irony lurking in his soft voice, and a chuckle that could so befool me?

"Well talk again, Haljan. You interest me - I've enjoyed it."

He sauntered away from me, joining the saturnine Ob Hahn, with whom presently I heard him discussing religion.

The arrest of Johnson had caused considerable discussion among the passengers. A few had seen me drag him forward to the cage. The incident had been the subject of discussion all afternoon. Captain Carter had posted a notice to the effect that Johnson's accounts had been found in serious error, and that Dr. Frank for this voyage would act in his stead.

* * * * *

It was near midnight when Snap and I closed and sealed the radio room and started for the chart room, where we were to meet with Captain Carter and the other officers. The passengers had nearly all retired. A game was in progress in the smoking room, but the deck was almost deserted.

Snap and I were passing along one of the interior corridors. The stateroom doors were all closed. The metal grid of the floor echoed our footsteps. Snap was in advance of me. His body suddenly rose in the air. He went like a balloon to the ceiling, struck it gently, and all in a heap came floating down and landed on the floor!

"What in the infernal -"

He was laughing as he picked himself up. But it was a brief laugh. We knew what had happened: the artificial gravity controls in the base of the ship, which by magnetic force gave us normality aboard, were being tampered with! For just this instant, this particular small section of this corridor had been cut off. The slight bulk of the *Planetara*, floating in space, had no appreciable gravity pull on Snap's body, and the impulse of his step as he came to the unmagnetized area of the corridor had thrown him to the ceiling. The area was normal now. Snap and I tested it gingerly.

He gripped me. "That never went wrong by accident, Gregg! Someone -"

We rushed to the nearest descending ladder. In the deserted lower room the bank of dials stood neglected. A score of dials and switches were here, governing the magnetism of different areas of the ship. There should have been a night operator, but he was gone.

Than we saw him lying nearby, sprawled, face down on the floor! In the silence and dim, lurid glow of the fluorescent tubes, we stood holding our breaths, peering and listening. No one here.

The guard was not dead. He lay unconscious from a blow on the head. A brawny fellow. We had him revived in a few moments. A broadcast flash of the call buzz brought Dr. Frank from the chart room.

"What's the matter?"

"Someone was here," I said hastily, "experimenting with the magnetic switches. Evidently unfamiliar with them - pulling one or another to test their workings and so see their reactions on the dials."

We told him what had happened to Snap in the corridor; the guard here was no worse off for the episode, save a lump on the head by an invisible assailant. We left him nursing his head, sitting belligerent at his post, alert to any danger and armed now with my heat-ray cylinder.

"Strange doings this voyage," he told us. "All the crew knows it. I'll stick it out now, but when we get back home I'm done with this star travelin'. I belong on the sea anyway."

We hurried back to the upper level. We would indeed have to plan something at this chart room conference. This was the first tangible attack our adversaries had made.

We were on the passenger deck headed for the chart room when all three of us stopped short, frozen with horror. Through the silent passenger quarters a scream rang out! A girl's shuddering, gasping scream. Terror in it. Horror. Or a scream of agony. In the silence of the dully vibrating ship it was utterly horrible.... It lasted an instant - a single long scream; then was abruptly stilled.

And with blood pounding my temples and rushing like ice through my veins, I recognized it.

Anita!

IX

"Good God, what was that?" Dr. Frank's face had gone white. Snap stood like a statue of horror.

The deck here was patched as always, with silver radiance from the deck ports. The empty deck chairs stood about. The scream was stilled, but now we heard a commotion inside - the rasp of opening cabin doors; questions from frightened passengers.

I found my voice. "Anita! Anita Prince!"

"Come on!" shouted Snap. "In her stateroom, A22!" He was dashing for the lounge archway.

Dr. Frank and I followed. I realized that we passed the deck door and window of A22. But they were dark, and evidently sealed on the inside. The dim lounge was in a turmoil; passengers standing at their cabin doors.

I shouted, "Go back to your rooms! We want order here - keep back!"

We came to the twin doors of A22 and A20. Both were closed. Dr. Frank was in advance of Snap and me now. He paused at the sound of Captain Carter's voice behind us.

"Was it from in there? Wait a moment!"

Carter dashed up. He had a large heat-ray projector in his hand. He shoved us aside. "Let me in first. Is the door sealed? Gregg, keep those passengers back!"

The door was not sealed. Carter burst into the room. I heard him gasp, "Good God!"

Snap and I shoved back three or four passengers. And in that instant Dr. Frank had been in the room and out again.

"There's been an accident! Get back, Gregg! Snap, help me keep the crowd away." He shoved me forcibly.

From within, Carter was shouting, "Keep them out! Where are you, Frank? Come back here! Send a flash for Balch!"

Dr. Frank went back into the room and banged the cabin door upon Snap and me. I was unarmed. Weapon in hand, Snap forced the panic-stricken passengers back to their rooms.

Snap reassured them glibly; but he knew no more about the facts than I. Moa, with a nightrobe drawn tight around her thin, tall figure, edged up to me.

"What has happened, *Set* Haljan?"

I gazed around for her brother Miko, but did not see him.

"An accident," I said shortly. "Go back to your room. Captain's orders."

She eyed me and then retreated. Snap was threatening everybody with his cylinder. Balch dashed up. "What in hell! Where is Carter?"

"In there." I pounded on A22. It opened cautiously. I could see only Carter, but I heard the murmuring voice of Dr. Frank through the interior connecting door to A20.

The Captain rasped, "Get out, Haljan! Oh, is that you, Balch? Come in." He admitted the older officer and slammed the door upon me again. And immediately reopened it.

"Gregg, keep the passengers quieted. Tell them everything's all right. Miss Prince got frightened - that's all. Then go to the turret. Tell Blackstone what's happened."

"But I don't know what's happened."

Carter was grim and white. He whispered, "I think it may turn out to be murder, Gregg! No, not dead yet.... Dr. Frank is trying ... don't stand there like an ass, man. Get to the turret! Verify our trajectory - no - wait...."

The Captain was almost incoherent. "Wait a minute. I don't mean that! Tell Snap to watch his radio room. Arm yourselves and guard our weapons."

I stammered, "If ... if she dies ... will you flash us word?"

He stared at me strangely. "I'll be there presently, Gregg."

He slammed the door upon me.

I followed his orders but it was like a dream of horror. The turmoil of the ship gradually quieted. Snap went to the radio room; Blackstone and I sat in the tiny chart room; how much time passed, I do not know. I was confused. Anita hurt! She might die ... murdered.... But why? By whom? Had George Prince been in his own room when the attack came? I thought now I recalled hearing the low murmur of his voice in there with Dr. Frank.

Where was Miko? It stabbed at me. I had not seen him among the passengers in the lounge.

Carter came into the chart room. "Gregg, you get to bed. You look like a ghost."

"But -"

"She's not dead. She may live. Dr. Frank and her brother are with her. They're doing all they can." He told us what had happened. Anita and George Prince had both been asleep, each in his respective room. Someone unknown had opened Anita's corridor door.

"Wasn't it sealed?"

"Yes. But the intruder opened it."

"Burst it? I didn't think it was broken."

"It wasn't broken. The assailant opened it somehow, and assaulted Miss Prince - shot her in the chest with a heat ray. Her left lung."

"Shot her?"

"Yes. But she did not see who did it. Nor did Prince. Her scream awakened him, but the intruder evidently fled out the corridor door of A22, the way he entered."

I stood weak and shaken at the chart room entrance. Anita - dying, perhaps; and all my dreams were fading into a memory of what might have been.

I was glad enough to get away. I would lie down for an hour and then go to Anita's stateroom. I'd demand that Dr. Frank let me see her.

I went to the stern deck where my cubby was located. My mind was confused but some instinct within me made me verify the seals of my door and window. They were intact. I entered cautiously, switched on the dimmer of the tube lights, and searched the room. It had only a bunk, my tiny desk, a chair and clothes robe. There was no evidence of any intruder here. I set my door and window alarm. Then I audiphoned to the radio room.

"Snap?"

"Yes."

I told him about Anita. Carter cut in on us from the chart room. "Stop that, you fools!"

We cut off. Fully dressed, I flung myself on my bed. Anita might die....

I must have fallen into a tortured sleep, I was awakened by the sound of my alarm buzzer. Someone was tampering with my door! Then the buzzer ceased; the marauder outside must have found a way of silencing it. But it had done its work - awakened me.

I had switched off the light; my cubby was Stygian black. A heat cylinder was in the bunk-bracket over my head. I searched for it, pried it loose softly.

I was fully awake. Alert. I could hear a faint sizzling - someone outside trying to unseal the door. In the darkness, cylinder in hand, I crept softly from the bunk. Crouched at the door. This time I would capture or kill this night prowler.

The sizzling was faintly audible. My door seal was breaking. Upon impulse I reached for the door, jerked it open.

No one there! The starlit segment of deck was empty. But I leaped and struck a solid body, crouching in the doorway. A giant man. Miko!

His electronized metallic robe burned my hands. I lunged against him - I was almost as surprised as he. I shot, but the stab of heat evidently missed him. The shock of my encounter, short-circuited his robe; he materialized in the starlight. A brief, savage encounter. He struck the weapon from my hand.

He had dropped his hydrogen torch, and tried to grip me. But I twisted away from his hold.

"So it's you!"

"Quiet, Gregg Haljan! I only want to talk."

Without warning, a stab of radiance shot from a weapon in his hand. It caught me. Ran like ice through my veins. Seized and numbed my limbs.

I fell helpless to the deck. Nerves and muscles paralyzed. My tongue was thick and inert. I could not speak, nor move. But I could see Miko bending over me, and hear him:

"I don't want to kill you, Haljan. We need you."

He gathered me up like a bundle in his huge arms; carried me swiftly across the deserted deck.

Snap's radio room in the network under the dome was diagonally overhead. A white actinic light shot from it - caught us, bathed us. Snap had been awake; had heard the commotion of our encounter.

His voice rang shrilly: "Stop! I'll shoot!" His warning siren rang out to alert the ship. His spotlight clung to us.

Miko ran with me a few steps. Then he cursed and dropped me; fled away. I fell like a sack of carbide to the deck. My senses faded into blackness....

"He's all right now."

I was in the chart room with Captain Carter, Snap and Dr. Frank bending over me. The surgeon said,

"Can you speak now, Gregg?"

I tried it. My tongue was thick, but it moved. "Yes." I was soon revived. I sat up, with Dr. Frank vigorously rubbing me.

"I'm all right." I told them what had happened.

Captain Carter said, "Yes, we know that. And it was Miko also whokilled Anita Prince. She told us before she died."

"Died!..." I leaped to my feet. "She ... died...."

"Yes, Gregg. An hour ago. Miko got into her stateroom and tried toforce his love upon her. She repulsed him. He killed her...."

It struck me blank. And then with a rush came the thought, "He says Miko killed her"....

I heard myself stammering, "Why - why we must get him!" I gathered my wits; a surge of hate swept me; a wild desire for vengeance.

"Why, by God, where is he? Why don't you go get him? I'll get him - I'll kill him!"

"Easy, Gregg!" Dr. Frank gripped me.

The Captain said gently. "We know how you feel, Gregg. She told us before she died."

"I'll bring him in here to you! But I'll kill him, I tell you!"

"No you won't, lad. We don't want him killed, not attacked, even. Not yet. We'll explain later."

They sat me down, calming me....

Anita dead. The door of the shining garden was closed. A brief glimpse given to me and to her of what might have been. And now she was dead....

X

I had not been able at first to understand why Captain Carter wanted Miko left at liberty. Within me there was that cry of vengeance, as though to strike Miko down would somehow lessen my own grief. Whatever Carter's purpose, Snap had not known it. But Balch and Dr. Frank were in the Captain's confidence - all three of them working on some plan of action.

It was obvious that at least two of our passengers were plotting with Miko and George Prince; trying on this voyage to learn what they could about Grantline's activities on the Moon - scheming doubtless to seize the treasure when the *Planetara* stopped at the Moon on the return voyage. I thought I could name those masquerading passengers. Ob Hahn, supposedly a Venus mystic. And Rance Rankin, who called himself an American magician. Those two, Snap and I agreed, seemed most suspicious. And there was the purser.

I sat for a time on the deck outside the chart room with Snap. Then Carter summoned us back, and we sat listening while he, Balch and Dr. Frank went on with their conference. Listening to them, I could not but agree that our best plan was to secure evidence which would incriminate all who were concerned in the plot. Miko, we were convinced, had been the Martian who followed Snap and me from Halsey's office in Greater New York. George Prince had doubtless been the invisible eavesdropper outside the radio room. He knew, and had told the others that Grantline had found that priceless metal on the

Moon and that the *Planetara* would stop there on the way home.

But we could not incarcerate George Prince for being an eavesdropper. Nor had we the faintest possible evidence against Ob Hahn or Rankin. And even the purser would probably be released by the Interplanetary Court of Ferrok-Shahn when it heard our evidence.

There was only Miko. We could arrest him for the murder of Anita. But if we did that now, the others would be put on their guard. It was Carter's idea to let Miko remain at liberty for a time and see if we could identify and incriminate his fellows. The murder of Anita obviously had nothing to do with any plot against Grantline Moon treasure.

"Why," exclaimed Balch, "there might be - probably are - huge Martian interests concerned in this thing. These men aboard are only emissaries, making this voyage to learn what they can. When they get to Ferrok-Shahn, they'll make their report, and then we'll have a real danger on our hands. Why, an outlaw ship could be launched from Ferrok-Shahn that would beat us back to the Moon - and Grantline is entirely without warning of any danger!"

It seemed obvious. Unscrupulous criminals in Ferrok-Shahn would be dangerous indeed, once these details of Grantline were given them. So now it was decided that in the remaining nine days of our outward voyage, we would attempt to secure enough evidence to arrest all these plotters.

"I'll have them all in the cage when we land," declared Carter grimly. "They'll make no report to their principals!"

Ah, the futile plans of men!

Yet, at the time, we thought it practical. We were all doubly armed now. Bullet projectors and heat ray cylinders. And we had several eavesdropping microphones which we planned to use whenever occasion offered.

Only twenty-eight hours of this eventful voyage had passed. The *Planetara* was some six million miles from the Earth; it blazed behind us, a tremendous giant.

The body of Anita was being made ready for burial. George Prince was still in his stateroom. Glutz, effeminate little hairdresser, who waxed rich acting as beauty doctor for the women passengers, and who, in his youth, had been an undertaker, had gone with Dr. Frank to prepare the body.

Gruesome details. I tried not to think of them. I sat, numbed, in the chart room.

An astronomical burial - there was little precedent for it. I dragged myself to the stern deck where, at five A.M., the ceremony took place.

We were a solemn little group, gathered there in the checkered starlight with the great vault of the heavens around us. A dismantled electronic projector - necessary when a long range gun was mounted - had been rigged up in one of the deck ports.

They brought out the body. I stood apart, gazing reluctantly at the small bundle, wrapped like a mummy in a dark metallic screen-cloth. A patch of black silk rested over her face. Four cabin stewards carried her; and beside her walked George Prince. A long black robe covered him, but his head was bare. And suddenly he reminded me of the ancient play-character of Hamlet. His black, wavy hair; his finely chiseled, pallid face, set now in a stern patrician cast. And staring, I realized that however much of the villain this man might be, at this instant, walking beside the body of his dead sister, he was stricken with grief. He loved that sister with whom he had lived since childhood; and to see him now no one could doubt it.

The little procession stopped in a patch of starlight by the port. They rested the body on a bank of chairs. The black-robed chaplain, roused from his bed and still trembling from excitement of this sudden, inexplicable death on board, said a brief, solemn little prayer. An appeal: That the Almighty Ruler of all these blazing worlds might guard the soul of this gentle girl whose mortal remains were now to be returned to Him.

Ah, if ever God seemed hovering close, it was now at this instant, on this starlit deck floating in the black void of space.

Then Carter for just a moment removed the black shroud from her face. I saw her brother gaze silently; saw him stoop and implant a kiss - and turn away. I did not want to look, but I found myself moving slowly forward.

She lay, so beautiful. Her face, white and calm and peaceful in death. My sight blurred.

"Easy Gregg," Snap was whispering to me. He had his arm around me. "Come on away."

They tied the shroud over her face. I did not see them as they put the body in the tube, sent it through the exhaust chamber and dropped it.

But a moment later I saw it, a small black, oblong bundle hovering beside us. It was perhaps a hundred feet away, circling us. Held by the *Planetara's* bulk, it had momentarily become our satellite. It swung around us like a moon. Gruesome satellite, by nature's laws forever to follow us.

Then from another tube at the bow, Blackstone operated a small zed-co-ray projector. Its dull light caught the floating bundle, neutralizing its metallic wrappings.

It swung off at a tangent. Speeding. Falling free in the dome of the heavens. A rotating black oblong. But in a moment distance dwindled it to a speck. A dull silver dot with the sunlight on it. A speck of human Earth dust, falling free....

It vanished. Anita - gone.

XI

I turned from the deck. Miko was near me! So he had dared show himself here among us! But I realized he could not be aware we knew he was the murderer. George Prince had been asleep, had not seen Miko with Anita. Miko, with impulsive rage had shot the girl and escaped. No doubt now he was cursing himself for having done it. And he could very well assume that Anita had died without regaining consciousness to tell who had killed her.

He gazed at me now. I thought for an instant he was coming over to talk with me. Though he probably considered he was not suspected of the murder of Anita, he realized, of course, that his attack on me was known. He must have wondered what action would be taken.

But he did not approach me. He moved away and went inside. Moa had been near him; and as though by prearrangement with him she now accosted me.

"I want to speak to you, *Set* Haljan."

"Go ahead."

I felt an instinctive aversion to this Martian girl. Yet she was not unattractive. Over six feet tall, straight and slim. Sleek blond hair. Rather a handsome face; not gray, like the burly Miko, but pink and white; stern lipped, but feminine, too. She was smiling gravely now.

Her blue eyes regarded me keenly. She said gently:

"A sad occurrence, Gregg Haljan. And mysterious. I would not question you -"

"Is that all you have to say?" I demanded.

"No. You are a handsome man, Gregg - attractive to women - to any Martian woman."

She said it impulsively. Admiration for me was on her face, in her eyes - a man cannot miss it.

"Thank you."

"I mean, I would be your friend. My brother Miko is so sorry about what happened between you and him this morning. He only wanted to talk to you, and he came to your cubby door -"

"With a torch to break its seal," I interjected.

She waved that away. "He was afraid you would not admit him. He told you he would not harm you."

"And so he struck me with one of your Martian paralyzing rays!"

"He is sorry...."

She seemed gauging me, trying, no doubt, to find out what reprisal would be taken against her brother. I felt sure that Moa was as active as a man in any plan that was under way to capture the Grantline treasure. Miko, with his ungovernable temper, was doing things that put their plans in jeopardy.

I demanded, "What did your brother want to talk to me about?"

"Me," she said surprisingly. "I sent him. A Martian girl goes after what she wants. Did you know that?"

She swung on her heel and left me. I puzzled over it. Was that why Miko struck me down and was carrying me off? I did not think so. I could not believe that all these incidents were so unrelated to what I knew was the main undercurrent They wanted me, had tried to capture me for something else.

Dr. Frank found me mooning alone. "Go to bed, Gregg. You look awful."

"I don't want to go to bed."

"Where's Snap?"

"I don't know. He was here a little while ago." I had not seen him since the burial of Anita.

"The Captain wants him," he said.

Within an hour the morning siren would arouse the passengers. I was seated in a secluded corner of the deck, when George Prince came along. He went past me, a slight, somber, dark-robed figure. He had on high, thick boots. A hood was over his head, but as he saw me he pushed it back and dropped down beside me.

For a moment he did not speak. His face showed pallid in the dim starlight.

"She said you loved her." His soft voice was throaty with emotion.

"Yes." I said it almost against my will. There seemed a bond springing between this bereaved brother and me. He added, so softly I could barely hear him: "That makes you, I think, almost my friend. And you thought you were my enemy."

I held my answer. An incautious tongue running under emotion is a dangerous thing. And I was sure of nothing.

He went on, "Almost my friend. Because - we both loved her, and she loved us both." He was hardly more than whispering. "And there is aboard one whom we both hate."

"Miko!" It burst from me.

"Yes. But do not say it."

Another silence fell between us. He brushed back the black curls from his forehead. "Have you an eavesdropping microphone, Haljan?"

I hesitated. "Yes."

"I was thinking...." He leaned closer. "If, in half an hour, you could use it upon Miko's cabin - I would rather tell you than anyone else. The cabin will be insulated, but I shall find a way of cutting off that insulation so that you can hear."

So George Prince had turned with us. The shock of his sister's death - himself allied with her murderer - had been too much for him. He was with us!

Yet his help must be given secretly. Miko would kill him instantly if it became known. He had been watchful of the deck. He stood up now.

"I think that is all."

As he turned away, I murmured, "But I do thank you...."

* * * * *

The name *Set* Miko glowed upon the door. It was in a transverse corridor similar to A22. The corridor was forward of the lounge: it opened off the small circular library.

The library was unoccupied and unlighted, dim with only the reflected lights from the nearby passages. I crouched behind a cylinder case. The door of Miko's room was in sight.

I waited perhaps five minutes. No one entered. Then I realized that doubtless the conspirators were already there. I set my tiny eavesdropper on the library floor beside me; connected its little battery; focused its projector. Was Miko's room insulated? I could not tell. There was a small ventilating grid above the door. Across its opening, if the room was insulated, a blue sheen of radiance would be showing. And there would be a faint hum. But from this distance I could not see or hear such details, and I was afraid to approach closer. Once in the transverse corridor, I would have no place to hide, no way of escape. If anyone approached Miko's door, I would be trapped.

I threw the current into my apparatus. I prayed, if it met interference, that the slight sound would pass unnoticed. George Prince had said that he would make opportunity to disconnect the room's insulation. He had evidently done so. I picked up the interior sounds at once; my headphone vibrated with them. And with trembling fingers on the little dial between my knees as I crouched in the darkness behind the cylinder case, I synchronized.

"Johnson is a fool." It was Miko's voice. "We must have the passwords."

"He got them from the radio room." A man's voice: I puzzled over it at first, then recognized it. Rance Rankin.

Miko said, "He is a fool. Walking around this ship as though with letters blazoned on his forehead, 'Watch me.... I need watching.' Hah! No wonder they apprehended him!"

Rankin's voice said: "He would have turned the papers over to us. I would not blame him too much. What harm -"

"Oh, I'll release him," Miko declared. "What harm? That

braying ass did us plenty of harm. He has lost the passwords. Better he had left them in the radio room."

Moa was in the room. Her voice said, "We've got to have them. The *Planetara*, upon such an important voyage as this, might be watched."

"No doubt it is," Rankin said quietly. "We ought to have the passwords. When we are in control of this ship...."

It sent a shiver through me. Were they planning to try and seize the *Planetara*? Now? It seemed so.

"Johnson undoubtedly memorized them," Moa was saying. "When we get him out -"

"Hahn is to do that, at the signal." Miko added, "George could do it better, perhaps."

And then I heard George Prince for the first time, "I'll try."

"No need," Miko said unexpectedly.

I could not see what had happened. A look, perhaps, which Prince could not avoid giving this man he had come to hate. Miko doubtless saw it, and the Martian's hot anger leaped.

Rankin said hurriedly, "Stop that!"

And Moa, "Let him alone, you fool! Sit down!"

I could hear the sound of a scuffle. A blow - a cry, half suppressed, from George Prince.

Then Miko: "I will not hurt him. Craven coward! Look at him! Hating me - frightened!"

I could fancy George Prince sitting there with murder in his heart, and Miko taunting him:

"Hates me now, because I shot his sister!"

Moa: "Hush!"

"I will not! Why should I not say it? I will tell you something else, George Prince. It was not Anita I shot at, but you! I meant nothing for her but love. If you had not interfered -"

This was different from what we had figured. George Prince had come in from his own room, had tried to rescue his sister, and in the scuffle, Anita had taken the shot instead of George.

"I did not even know I had hit her," Miko was saying. "Not until I heard she was dead." He added sardonically, "I hoped it was you I had hit, George. And I will tell you this: you hate me no more than I hate you. If it were not for your knowledge of ores -"

"Is this to be a personal wrangle?" Rankin interrupted. "I thought we were here to plan -"

"It is planned," Miko said shortly. "I give orders, I do not plan. I am waiting now for the moment -" He checked himself.

Moa said, "Does Rankin understand that no harm is to come to Gregg Haljan?"

"Yes," Rankin said. "And Dean. We need them, of course. But you cannot make Dean send messages if he refuses, nor make Haljan navigate."

"I know enough to check on them," Miko said grimly. "They will not fool me. And they will obey me, have no fear. A little touch of sulphuric -" His laugh was gruesome. "It makes the most stubborn, very willing."

"I wish," said Moa, "we had Haljan safely hidden. If he is hurt - killed -"

So that was why Miko had tried to capture me? To keep me safe so that I might navigate the ship.

It occurred to me that I should get Carter at once. A plot to seize the *Planetara* - but when?

I froze with startled horror.

The diaphragms at my ears rang with Miko's words: "I have set the time for now - two minutes -"

It seemed to startle Rankin and George Prince as much as it did me. Both exclaimed: "No!"

"No? Why not? Everyone is at his post!"

Prince repeated, "No!"

And Rankin, "But can we trust them? The stewards - the crew?"

"Eight of them are our own men! You didn't know that, Rankin? They've been aboard the *Planetara* for several voyages. Oh, this is no quickly planned affair, even though we let you in on it so recently. You and Johnson.... By God!"

There was a commotion in the stateroom. I crouched, tense. Miko had discovered that his insulation had been cut off! He had evidently leaped to his feet. I heard a chair overturn. And the Martian's roar: "It's off! Did you do that, Prince? By God, if I thought -"

My apparatus went suddenly dead as Miko flung on his insulation. I lost my wits in the confusion: I should have instantly taken off my vibrations. There was interference: it showed in the dark space of the ventilator grid over Miko's doorway, a snapping in the air, there - a swirl of sparks.

I heard with my unaided ears Miko's roar over his insulation:

"By God, they're listening!"

The scream of hand sirens sounded from his stateroom. It rang over the ship. His signal! I heard it answered from some distant point. And then a shot: a commotion in the lower corridors....

The attack upon the *Planetara* had begun!

I was on my feet. The shouts of startled passengers sounded, a turmoilbeginning everywhere.

I stood momentarily transfixed. The door of Miko's stateroom burst open. He stood there, with Rankin, Moa and George Prince crowding him.

He saw me. "You, Gregg Haljan!"

He came leaping at me.

XII

I was taken wholly by surprise. There was an instant when I stood numbed, fumbling for a weapon at my belt, undecided whether to run or stand my ground. Miko was no more than twenty feet from me. He checked his forward rush. The light from an overhead tube was on him: I saw in his hand the cylinder projector of his paralyzing ray.

I plucked my heat cylinder from my belt, and fired without taking aim. My tiny heat beam flashed. I must have grazed Miko's hand. His roar of anger and pain rang out over the turmoil. He dropped his weapon; then stooped to pick it up. But Moa forestalled him. She leaped and seized it.

"Careful! Fool, you promised not to harm him!"

A confusion of swift action. Rankin had turned and darted away. I saw George Prince stumbling half in front of the struggling Miko and Moa. And I heard footsteps beside me. A hand gripped me, jerked at me.

Over the turmoil, Prince's voice sounded: "Gregg Haljan!"

I recall that I had the impression that Prince was frightened; he had half fallen in front of Miko. And there was Miko's voice: "Let go of me!"

It was Balch gripping me. "Gregg! This way - run! Get out of here! He'll kill you with that ray!"

Miko's ray flashed, but George Prince had knocked his arm. I did not dare fire again. Prince was in the way. Balch, who was unarmed, shoved me violently back.

"Gregg! The chart room!"

I turned and ran, with Balch after me. Prince had fallen or been felled by Miko. A flash followed me from Miko's weapon, but again it missed. He did not pursue me. Instead he ran the other way, through the portside door of the library.

Balch and I found ourselves in the library. Shouting, frightened passengers were everywhere. The place was in wild confusion, the whole ship ringing now with shouts.

"To the chart room, Gregg!"

I called to the passengers, "Go back to your rooms!"

I followed Balch. We ran through the archway to the deck. In the starlight I saw figures scurrying aft, but none were near us. The deck forward was dim with heavy shadows. The oval windows and door of the chart room were blue-yellow from the tube lights inside. No one seemed on the deck there. And then as we approached, I saw further forward in the bow, the trap door to the cage standing open. Johnson had been released.

From one of the chart room windows a heat ray sizzled. It barely missed us. Balch shouted, "Carter - don't!"

The Captain called, "Oh you, Balch - and Haljan -"

He came out on the deck as we rushed up. His left arm was dangling limp.

"God - this -" He got no further. From the turret overhead a tiny search beam came down and disclosed us. Blackstone was supposed to be on duty up there, with a course master at the controls. But, glancing up, I saw, illumined by the turret lights, the figure of Ob Hahn in his purple-white robe, and Johnson, the purser. And on the turret balcony, two fallen men - Blackstone and the course master.

Johnson was training the spotlight on us. And Hahn fired a Martian ray. It struck Balch beside me. He dropped.

Carter was shouting, "Inside - Gregg! Get inside!"

I stopped to raise up Balch. Another beam came down. A heat ray this time. It caught the fallen Balch full on the chest, piercing him through. The smell of his burning flesh rose to sicken me. He was dead. I dropped his body. Carter shoved me into the chart room.

In the small, steel-lined room, Carter and I slid the door closed. We were alone here. The thing had come so quickly it had taken Captain Carter, like us all, wholly unawares. We had anticipated spying eavesdroppers, but not this open brigandage. No more than a minute or two had passed since Miko's siren in his stateroom had given the signal for attack. Carter had been in the chart room. Blackstone was in the turret. At the outbreak of confusion, Carter dashed out to see Hahn releasing Johnson from the cage. From the forward chart room window now I could see where Hahn with a torch had broken the cage seal. The torch lay on the deck. There had been an exchange of shots; Carter's arm was paralyzed; Johnson and Hahn had escaped.

Carter was as confused as I. There had simultaneously been an encounter up in the turret. Blackstone and the course master were killed. The lookout had been shot from his post in the forward observatory. The body dangled now, twisted half in and half out the window.

We could see several of Miko's men - erstwhile members of our crew and steward corps - scurrying from the turret along the upper bridge toward the dark and silent radio room. Snap was up there. But was he? The radio room glowed suddenly with dim light, but there was no evidence of a fight there. The fighting seemed mostly below the deck, down in the hull corridors. A blended horror of sounds came up to us. Screams, shouts and the hissing and snapping of ray weapons. Our crew - such of them as were loyal - were making a stand below. But it was brief. Within a minute it died away. The passengers, amidships in the superstructure, were still shouting. Then above them Miko's roar sounded.

"Be quiet! Go in your rooms - you will not be harmed."

The brigands in these few minutes were in control of the ship. All but this little chart room, where, with most of the ship's weapons, Carter and I were entrenched.

"God, Gregg, that this should come upon us!"

Carter was fumbling with the chart room weapons. "Here, Gregg. Help me. What have you got? Heat ray? That's all I had ready."

It struck me then as I helped him make the connections that Carter in this crisis was at best an inefficient commander. His red face had gone splotchy purple; his hands were trembling. Skilled as Captain of a peaceful liner, he was at a loss now. But I could not blame him. It is easy to say we might have taken warning, done this or that, and come triumphant through the attack. But only the fool looks backward and says, "I would have done better."

I tried to summon my wits. The ship was lost to us unless Carter and I could do something. Our futile weapons! They were all here - four or five heat ray hand projectors that could send a pencil ray a hundred feet or so. I shot one diagonally up at the turret where Johnson was leering down at our rear window, but he saw my gesture and dropped back out of sight. The heat beam flashed harmlessly up and struck the turret room. Then across the turret window came a sheen of radiance

- an electrobarrage. And behind it, Hahn's suave, evil face appeared. He shouted down:

"We have orders to spare you, Gregg Haljan - or you would have been killed long ago!"

My answering shot hit his barrage with a shower of sparks, behind which he stood unmoved.

Carter handed me another weapon. "Gregg, try this."

I leveled the old explosive projector; Carter crouched beside me. But before I could press the trigger, from somewhere down the starlit deck an electro beam hit me. The little rifle exploded, broke its breech. I sank back to the floor, tingling from the shock of the hostile current. My hands were blackened from the exploded powder.

Carter seized me. "No use. Hurt?"

"No."

The stars through the dome windows were swinging. A long swing - the shadows and patterns on the starlit deck were all shifting. The *Planetara* was turning. The heavens revolved in a great round sweep of movement, then settled as we took our new course.

Hahn at the turret controls had swung us. The Earth and the Sun showed over our bow quarter. The sunlight mingled red-yellow with the brilliant starlight. Hahn's signals were sounding; I heard them answered from the mechanism rooms down below. Brigands there - in full control. The gravity plates were being set to the new positions: We were on our new course. Headed a point or two off the Earthline. Not headed for the Moon? I wondered.

Carter and I were planning nothing. What was there to plan? We were under observation. A Martian paralyzing ray - or an electronic beam, far more deadly than our own puny weapons - would have struck us the instant we tried to leave the chart room.

My thoughts were interrupted by a shout from down the deck. At a corner of the cabin superstructure some fifty feet from our windows the figure of Miko appeared. A radiance barrage hung about him like a shimmering mantle. His voice sounded: "Gregg Haljan, do you yield?"

Carter leaped up from where he and I were crouching. Against all reason of safety he leaned from the low window, waving his hamlike fist.

"Yield? No! I am in command here, you pirate! Brigand - murderer!"

I dragged him back sharply. "For God's sake -"

He was spluttering; and over it Miko's sardonic laugh sounded. "Shall we argue about it?"

I stood up. "What do you want to say, Miko?"

Behind him the tall, thin figure of his sister showed. She was plucking at him. He turned violently. "I won't harm him! Gregg Haljan - is this a truce? You will not shoot?" He was shielding Moa.

"No," I called. "For a moment, no. A truce. What is it you want to say?"

I could hear the babble of passengers who were herded in the cabin with brigands guarding them. George Prince, bare-headed, but shrouded in his cloak, showed in a patch of light behind Moa. He looked my way and then retreated.

Miko called, "You must yield. We want you, Haljan."

"No doubt," I jeered.

"Alive. It is easy to kill you."

I could not doubt that. Carter and I were little more than rats in a trap. But Miko wanted to take me alive: that was not so simple. He added persuasively:

"We want you to navigate us. Will you?"

"No."

"Will you help us, Captain Carter? Tell your cub, this Haljan, to yield."

Carter roared, "Get back from there. There is no truce!"

I shoved aside his leveled projector. "Wait a minute, Miko. Navigate where?"

"That is our business. When you come out here, I will give you the course."

I realized that all this parley was a ruse of Miko's to take me alive. He had made a gesture. Hahn, watching him from the turret window, doubtless flashed a signal down to the hull corridors. The magnetizer control under the chart room was altered, our artificial gravity cut off. I felt the sudden lightness: I gripped the window casement and clung. Carter was startled into incautious movement. It flung him out into the room, his arms and legs flailing.

And across the chart room, in the opposite window, I felt rather than saw the shape of something. A figure, almost invisible but not quite, was trying to climb in! I flung the empty rifle I was holding. It hit something solid in the window. In a flare of sparks a blackhooded figure materialized. A man climbing in! His weapon spat. There was a tiny electronic flash, deadly silent. The intruder had shot at Carter:

struck him. Carter gave one queer scream. He had floated to the floor; his convulsive movement when he was hit hurled him to the ceiling. His body struck; twitched; bounced back and sank inert on the floor grid almost at my feet.

I clung to the casement. Across the room of the weightless room the hooded intruder was also clinging. His hood fell back. It was Johnson.

"Killed him, the bully! Now for you, Mr. Third Officer Haljan!"

But he did not dare fire at me. Miko had forbidden it. I saw him reach under his robe, doubtless for a low-powered paralyzing ray. But he never got it out. I had no weapon within reach. I leaned into the room, still holding the casement, and doubled my legs under me. I kicked out from the window.

The force catapulted me across the space across the room like a volplane. I struck the purser. We gripped. Our locked, struggling bodies bounced out into the room. We struck the floor, surged up like balloons to the ceiling, struck it with a flailing arm or leg and floated back.

Grotesque, abnormal combat! Like fighting in weightless water. Johnson clutched his weapon, but I twisted his wrist, held his arm outstretched so that he could not aim it. I was aware of Miko's voice shouting on the deck outside.

Johnson's left hand was gouging at my face, his fingers digging at my eyes. We lunged down.

I twisted his wrists. He dropped the weapon and it sank away, I tried to reach it but could not.... Then I had him by the throat. I was stronger than he, and more agile. I tried choking him, I had his thick bull neck within my fingers. He kicked, scrambled, tore and gouged at me. Tried to shout, but it ended in a gurgle. And then, as he felt his breath stopped, his hands came up in an effort to tear mine loose.

We sank again to the floor. We were momentarily upright. I felt my feet touch. I bent my knees. We sank further. And then I kicked violently upward. Our locked bodies shot to the ceiling. Johnson's head was above me. It struck the steel roof of the chart room. A violent blow. I felt him go suddenly limp. I cast him off and, doubling my body, I kicked at the ceiling. It sent me diagonally downward to the window, where I clung.

And I saw Miko standing on the deck with a weapon leveled at me!

XIII

"Haljan! Yield or I'll fire! Moa, give me the smaller one."

He had in his hand too large a projector. Its ray would kill me. If he wanted to take me alive, he would not fire. I chanced it.

"No!" I tried to draw myself beneath the window. An automatic projector was on the floor where Carter had dropped it. I pulled myself down. Miko did not fire. I reached the weapon. The bodies of the Captain and Johnson had drifted together on the floor in the center of the room.

I hitched myself back to the window. With upraised weapon I gazed cautiously out. Miko had disappeared. The deck within my line of vision, was empty.

But was it? Something told me to beware. I clung to the casement, ready upon the instant to shove myself down. There was a movement in a shadow along the deck. Then a figure rose up.

"Don't fire, Haljan!"

The sharp command, half appeal, stopped the pressure of my finger. It was the tall, lanky Englishman. Sir Arthur Coniston, he as called himself. So he too, was one of Miko's band! The light through a dome window fell full on him.

"If you fire, Haljan, and kill me - Miko will kill you then, surely."

From where he had been crouching he could not command my window. But now, upon the heels of his placating words, he abruptly shot. The low-powered ray, had it struck, would have felled me without killing me. But it went over my head as I dropped. Its aura made my senses reel.

Coniston shouted, "Haljan!"

I did not answer. I wonder if he would dare approach to see if I had been hit. A minute passed. Then another. I thought I heard Miko's voice on the deck outside. But it was an aerial, microscopic whisper close beside me.

"We see you, Haljan. You must yield!"

Their eavesdropping vibrations, with audible projection, were upon me. I retorted loudly, "Come and get me! You cannot take me alive!"

I do protest if this action of mine in the chart room may seem bravado. I had no wish to die. There was within me a very healthy desire for life. But I felt, by holding out, that some chance might come wherewith I might turn events against these brigands. Yet reason told me it was hopeless. Our loyal members of the crew were killed, no doubt. Captain Carter and Balch were dead. The lookouts and course masters, also. And Blackstone.

There remained only Dr. Frank and Snap. Their fate I did not yet know. And there was George Prince. He, perhaps, would help me if he could. But, at best, he was a dubious ally.

"You are very foolish, Haljan," murmured Miko's voice. And then I heard Coniston:

"See here, why would not a hundred pounds of gold leaf tempt you? The code words which were taken from Johnson - I mean to say, why not tell us where they are?"

So that was one of the brigands' new difficulties! Snap had taken the code word sheet that time we sealed the purser in the cage.

I said, "You'll never find them. And when a police ship sights us, what will you do then?"

The chances of a police ship were slight indeed, but the brigands evidently did not know that. I wondered again what had become of Snap. Was he captured or still holding them off?

I was watching my windows; for at any moment, under the cover of talk, I might be assailed.

Gravity came suddenly to the room. Miko's voice said: "We mean well by you, Haljan. There is your normality. Join us. We need you to chart our course."

"And a hundred pounds of gold leaf," urged Coniston. "Or more. Why, this treasure -"

I could hear an oath from Miko. And then his ironic voice. "We will not bother you, Haljan. There is no hurry. You will be hungry in good time. And sleepy. Then we will come and get you. And a little acid will help you to think differently about us...."

His vibrations died away. The pull of gravity in the room was normal. I was alone in the dim silence, with the bodies of Carter and Johnson huddled on the grid. I bent to examine them. Both were dead.

My isolation was not ruse this time. The outlaws made no further attack. Half an hour passed. The deck outside, what I could see of it, was vacant. Balch lay dead close outside the chart room door. The bodies of Blackstone and the course master had been removed from the turret window. As a forward lookout, one of Miko's men was on duty in the nearby tower. Hahn was at the turret's controls. The ship was under orderly handling, heading back upon a new course. For the Earth? The Moon? It did not seem so.

I found, in the chart room, a Benson curve light projector which poor Captain Carter had nearly assembled. I worked on it, trained it through my rear window along the empty deck; bent it into the lounge archway. Upon my grid the image of the lounge interior presently focused. The passengers in the lounge were huddled in a group. Disheveled, frightened, with Moa standing watching them. Stewards were serving them with a meal.

Upon a bench, bodies were lying. Some were dead. I saw Rance Rankin. Others were evidently only injured. Dr. Frank was moving among them, attending them. Venza was there, unharmed. And I saw the gamblers, Shac and Dud, sitting white-faced, whispering together. And Glutz's little beribboned, becurled figure on a stool.

George Prince was there, standing against the wall, shrouded in his mourning cloak, watching the scene with alert, roving eyes. And by the opposite doorway, the huge towering figure of Miko stood on guard. But Snap was missing.

A brief glimpse. Miko saw my Benson light. I could have equipped a heat ray and fired along the curved Benson light into that lounge. But Miko gave me no time.

He slid the lounge door closed, and Moa leaped to close the one on my side. My grid showed only the blank deck and door.

Another interval. I had made plans. Futile plans! I could get into the turret perhaps, and kill Hahn. I had the invisible cloak which Johnson was wearing. I took it from his body. Its mechanism could be repaired. Why, with it I could creep about the ship, kill these brigands one by one, perhaps. George Prince would be with me. The brigands who had been posing as the stewards and crew members were unable to navigate; they would obey my orders. There were only Miko, Coniston and Hahn to kill.

From my window I could gaze up to the radio room. And now, abruptly, I heard Snap's voice: "No! I tell you - no!"

And Miko, "Very well, then. We'll try this."

So Snap was captured but not killed. Relief swept me. He was in the radio room and Miko was with him. But my relief was short-lived. After a brief interval, there came a moan from Snap. It floated down the silence overhead and made me shudder.

My Benson beam shot into the radio room. It showed me Snap lying there on the floor. He was bound with wire. His torso had been stripped. His livid face was ghastly plain in my light.

Miko was bending over him. Miko with a heat cylinder no longer than a finger. Its needle beam played upon Snap's naked chest. I could see the gruesome little trail of smoke rising; and as Snap twisted and jerked, there on his flesh was the red and blistered trail of the violet ray.

"Now will you tell?"

"No!"

Miko laughed. "No? Then I shall write my name a little deeper...."

A black sear now - a trail etched in the quivering flesh.

"Oh!" Snap's face went white as chalk as he pressed his

lips together.

"Or a little acid? This fire-writing does not really hurt? Tell me what you did with those code words!"

"No!"

In his absorption Miko did not notice my light. Nor did I have the wit to try and fire along it. I was trembling. Snap under torture!

As the beam went deeper. Snap suddenly screamed. But he ended, "No! I will send no message for you -"

It had been only a moment. In the chart room window beside me again a figure appeared! No image. A solid, living person, undisguised by any cloak of invisibility. George Prince had chanced my fire and crept upon me.

"Haljan! Don't attack me."

I dropped my light connections. As impulsively I stood up, I saw through the window the figure of Coniston on the deck watching the result of Prince's venture.

"Haljan - yield."

Prince no more than whispered it. He stood outside on the deck; the low window casement touched his waist. He leaned over it.

"He's torturing Snap! Call out that you will yield."

The thought had already been in my mind. Another scream from Snap filled me with horror. I shouted, "Miko! Stop!"

I rushed to the window and Prince gripped me. "Louder!"

I called louder: "Miko! Stop!" My upflung voice mingled with

Snap's agony of protest. Then Miko heard me. His head and shoulders showed up there at the radio room oval.

"You - Haljan?"

Prince shouted, "I have made him yield. He will obey you if you stop that torture."

I think that poor Snap must have fainted. He was silent. I called, "Stop! I will do what you command."

Miko jeered, "That is good. A bargain, if you and Dean obey me. Disarm him, Prince, and bring him out."

Miko moved back into the radio room. On the deck, Coniston was advancing, but cautiously mistrustful of me.

"Gregg."

George Prince flung a leg over the casement and leaped lightly into the dim chart room. His small slender figure stood beside me, clung to me.

A moment, while we stood there together. No ray was upon us. Coniston could not see us, nor could he hear our whispers.

"Gregg."

A different voice; its throaty, husky quality gone. A soft pleading. "Gregg - Gregg, don't you know me? Gregg, dear...."

Why, what was this? Not George Prince? A masquerader, yet so like George Prince.

"Gregg don't you know me?"

Clinging to me. A soft touch upon my arm. Fingers, clinging. A surge of warm, tingling current was flowing between us.

My sweep of instant thoughts. A speck of human Earth dust falling free. That was George Prince who had been killed. George Prince's body, disguised by the scheming Carter and Dr. Frank, buried in the guise of his sister. And this black-robed figure who was trying to help me....

"Anita! Anita darling -"

"Gregg, dear one!"

"Anita!" My arms went around her, my lips pressed hers, and felt her tremulous eager answer.

The form of Coniston showed at our window. She cast me off. She said, with her throaty swagger of amused, masculinity:

"I have him, Sir Arthur. He will obey us."

I sensed her warning glance. She shoved me toward the window. She said ironically, "Have no fear, Haljan. You will not be tortured, you and Dean, if you obey our commands."

Coniston gripped me. "You fool! You caused us a lot of trouble. Move along there!"

He jerked me roughly through the window. Marched me the length of the deck, out to the stern space, opened the door of my cubby, flung me in and sealed the door upon me.

"Miko will come presently."

I stood in the darkness of my tiny room, listening to his retreating footsteps. But my mind was not upon him.

All the universe, in that instant, had changed for me. Anita was alive!

XIV

The giant Miko stood confronting me. He slid my cubby door closed behind him. He stood with his head towering close against my ceiling. His cloak was discarded. In his leather clothes, and with his clanking sword ornament, his aspect carried the swagger of a brigand of old. He was bare-headed; the light from one of my tubes fell upon his grinning, leering gray face.

"So, Gregg Haljan? You have come to your senses at last. You do not wish me to write my name on your chest? I would not have done that to Dean; he forced me. Sit back."

I had been on my bunk. I sank back at the gesture of his huge hairy arm. His forearm was bare now; the sear of a burn on it was plain to be seen. He remarked my gaze.

"True. You did that, Haljan, in Greater New York. But I bear you no malice. I want to talk to you now."

He cast about for a seat, and took the little stool which stood by my desk. His hand held a small cylinder of the Martian paralyzing ray. He rested it beside him on the desk.

"Now we can talk."

I remained silent. Alert. Yet my thoughts were whirling. Anita was alive. Masquerading as her brother. And, with the joy of it, came a shudder. Above everything, Miko must not know.

"A great adventure we are upon, Haljan."

My thoughts came back. Miko was talking with an assumption of friendly comradeship. "All is well - and we need you, as I have said before. I am no fool. I have been aware of everything that went on aboard this ship. You, of all the officers, are most clever at the routine mathematics. Is that so?"

"Perhaps."

"You are modest." He fumbled at a pocket of his jacket, produced a scroll-sheaf. I recognized it. Blackstone's figures. The calculation Blackstone made of the asteroid we had passed.

"I am interested in these," Miko went on. "I want you to verify them. And this." He held up another scroll. "This is the calculation of our present position and our course. Hahn claims he is a navigator. We have set the ship's gravity plates - see, like this."

He handed me the scrolls. He watched me keenly as I glanced over them.

"Well?" I said.

"You are sparing of words, Haljan. By the devils of the airways, I could make you talk! But I want to be friendly."

I handed him back the scrolls. I stood up. I was almost within reach of his weapon, but with a sweep of his great arm he knocked me back to my bunk.

"You dare?" Then he smiled. "Let us not come to blows!"

In truth, physical violence could get me nothing. I would have to try guile. And I saw now that his face was flushed and his eyes unnaturally bright. He had been drinking alcolite; not enough to befuddle him, but enough to make him triumphantly talkative.

"Hahn may not be much of a mathematician," I suggested. "But there is your Sir Arthur Coniston." I managed a sarcastic grin. "Is that his name?"

"Almost. Haljan, will you verify these figures?"

"Yes. But why? Where are we going?"

He laughed. "You are afraid I will not tell you! Why should I? This great adventure of mine is progressing perfectly. A tremendous stake, Haljan. A hundred million dollars in gold leaf. There will be fabulous riches for all of us -"

"But where are we going?"

"To that asteroid," he said. "I must get rid of these passengers. I am no murderer."

With a half-dozen killings in the recent fight this was hardly convincing. But he was obviously wholly serious. He seemed to read my thoughts.

"I kill only when necessary. We will land upon the asteroid. A perfect place to maroon the passengers. Is it not so? I will give them the necessities of life. They will be able to signal. And in a month or so, when we are perfectly safe and finished with our adventure, a police ship no doubt will rescue them."

"And then, from the asteroid," I suggested, "we are going -"

"To the Moon, Haljan. What a clever guesser you are! Coniston and Hahn are calculating our course. But I have no great confidence in them. And so I want you."

"You have me."

"Yes. I have you. I would have killed you long ago - I am an impulsive fellow - but my sister restrained me."

He gazed at me slyly. "Moa seems strangely to like you, Haljan."

"Thanks," I said. "I'm flattered."

"She still hopes I may really win you to join us," he went on. "Gold leaf is a wonderful thing; there would be plenty for you in this affair. And to be rich, and have the love of a woman like Moa...."

He paused. I was trying cautiously to gauge him, to get from him all the information I could. I said, with another smile, "That is premature, to talk of Moa. I will help you chart your course. But this venture, as you call it, is dangerous. A police ship -"

"There are not many," he declared. "The chances of our encountering one are very slim." He grinned at me. "You know that as well as I do. And we now have those code passwords - I forced Dean to tell me where he had hidden them. If we should be challenged, our password answer will relieve suspicion."

"The *Planetara*," I objected, "being overdue at Ferrok-Shahn, will cause alarm. You'll have a covey of patrol ships after you."

"That will be two weeks from now," he smiled. "I have a ship of my own in Ferrok-Shahn. It lies there waiting now, manned and armed. I am hoping that, with Dean's help, we may be able to flash them a signal. It will join us on the Moon. Fear not for the danger, Haljan. I have great interests allied with me in this thing. Plenty of money. We have planned carefully."

He was idly fingering his cylinder; he gazed at me as I sat docile on my bunk. "Did you think George Prince was a leader of this? A mere boy. I engaged him a year ago - his knowledge of science is valuable to us."

My heart was pounding but I strove not to show it. He went on calmly.

"I told you I am impulsive. Half a dozen times I have nearly killed George Prince, and he knows it." He frowned. "I wish I had killed him instead of his sister. That was an error."

There was a note of real concern in his voice. He added, "That is done - nothing can change it. George Prince is helpful to me. Your friend Dean, is another. I had trouble with him, but he is docile now."

I said abruptly, "I don't know whether your promise means anything or not, Miko. But Prince said you would use no more torture."

"I won't. Not if you and Dean obey me."

"You tell Dean I have agreed to that. You say he gave you the code words he took from Johnson?"

"Yes. There was a fool, for you! That Johnson! You blame me, Haljan, for the death of Carter? You need not. Johnson offered to try and capture you, take you both alive. He killed Carter because he was angry with him. A stupid, vengeful fool! He is dead and I'm glad of it."

My mind was on Miko's plans. I ventured, "This treasure on the Moon - did you say it was on the Moon?"

"Don't play the fool," he retorted. "I know as much about Grantline as you do."

"That's very little."

"Perhaps."

"Perhaps you know more, Miko. The Moon is a big place. Where, for instance, is Grantline located?"

I held my breath. Would he tell me that? A score of questions - vague plans were in my mind. How skilled at mathematics were these brigands? Miko, Coniston, Hahn - could I fool them? If I could learn Grantline's location on the Moon, and keep the *Planetara* away from it. A pretended error of charting. Time lost - and perhaps Snap could find an opportunity to signal Earth, get help.

Miko answered my question as bluntly as I asked it. "I don't know where Grantline is located. But we will find out. He will not suspect the *Planetara* so when we get close to the Moon, we will signal and ask him. We can trick him into telling us. You think I do not know what is on your mind, Haljan? There is a secret code of signals arranged between Dean and Grantline. I have forced Dean to confess it. Without torture! Prince helped me in that. He persuaded Dean not to defy me. A very persuasive fellow, George Prince. More diplomatic than I am. I give him credit for that."

I strove to hold my voice calm. "If I should join you, Miko - my word, if I ever gave it, you would find dependable - I would say George Prince is very valuable to us. You should rein your temper. He is half your size - you might some time, without intention, do him injury."

He laughed. "Moa says so. But have no fear -"

"I was thinking," I persisted. "I'd like to have a talk with George Prince."

Ah, my pounding, tumultuous heart! But I was smiling calmly. And I tried to put into my voice a shrewd note of cupidity. "I really know very little about this treasure, Miko. If there were a million or two of gold leaf in it for me -"

"Perhaps there would be."

"Suppose you let me have a talk with Prince? I have some scientific knowledge myself about the powers of this catalyst.

Prince's knowledge and mine - we might be able to come to a calculation on the value of Grantline's treasure. You don't know. You are only assuming."

I paused after this glib outburst. Whatever may have been in Miko's mind, I cannot say. But abruptly he stood up. I had left my bunk but he waved me back.

"Sit down. I am not like Moa. I would not trust you just because you protested you would be loyal." He picked up his cylinder. "We will talk again." He gestured to the scrolls he had left upon my desk. "Work on those. I will judge you by the results."

He was no fool, this brigand leader.

"Yes," I agreed. "You want a true course to the asteroid?"

"Yes. And by the gods, I warn you, I can check up on you!"

I said meekly, "Very well. But you ask Prince if he wants my calculations on Grantline's possibilities."

I shot Miko a foxy look as he stood by the door. I added, "You think you are clever. There is plenty you don't know. Our first night out from Earth - Grantline's signals - didn't it ever occur to you that I might have some figures on his treasure?"

It startled him. "Where are they?"

I tapped my forehead. "You don't suppose I was foolish enough to record them. You ask Prince if he wants to talk to me. A hundred million, or two hundred million - it would make a big difference, Miko."

"I will think about it." He backed out and sealed the door upon me.

But Anita did not come. I verified Hahn's figures, which were very nearly correct. I charted a course for the asteroid; it was almost the one which had been set.

Coniston came for my results. "I say, we are not so bad as navigators, are we? I think we're jolly good, considering our inexperience. Not bad at all, eh?"

"No."

I did not think it wise to ask him about Prince.

"Are you hungry, Haljan?"

"Yes."

A steward came with a meal. The saturnine Hahn stood at my door with a weapon upon me while I ate. They were taking no chances and they were wise not to.

The day passed. Day and night, all the same of aspect here in the starry vault of space. But with the ship's routine it was day. And then another time of sleep. I slept fitfully, worrying, trying to plan. Within a few hours we would be nearing the asteroid.

The time of sleep was nearly passed. My chronometer marked five A.M. original Earth starting time. The seal of my cubby door hissed. The door slowly opened.

Anita!

She stood there with her cloak around her. A distance away on the shadowed deck Coniston was loitering.

"Anita!" I whispered it.

"Gregg, dear!"

She turned and gestured to the watching brigand. "I will not be long, Coniston."

She came in and half closed the door upon us, leaving it open enough so that we could make sure that Coniston did not advance.

I stepped back where he could not see us. "Anita!"

She flung herself into my opened arms.

XV

A moment when, beyond the thought of the nearby brigand - or the possibility of an eavesdropping ray trained now upon my cubby - a moment while Anita and I held each other, and whispered those things which could mean nothing to the world, but which were all the world to us!

Then it was she whose wits brought us back from the shining fairyland of our love, into the sinister reality of the *Planetara*.

"Gregg, if they are listening -"

I pushed her away. This brave little masquerader! Not for my life, or for all the lives on the ship, would I consciously have endangered her.

"But Grantline's findings!" I said aloud. "In his message - see here, Prince -"

Coniston was too far away on the deck to hear us. Anita went to my door again and waved at him reassuringly. I put my ear to the door opening and listened at the space across the grid of the ventilator over my bunk. The hum of a vibration would have been audible at those two points. But there was nothing.

"It's all right," I whispered, and she clung to me - so small beside me. With the black robe thrown aside, it seemed that I could not miss the curves of her woman's figure. A dangerous game she was playing. Her hair had been cut short to the base of her neck, in the fashion of her dead brother. Her eyelashes had been clipped: the line of her brows altered. And now, in the light of my tube as it shone upon her earnest face, I could remark other changes. Glutz, the little beauty specialist, was in this secret. With plastic skill he had altered the set of her jaw - put masculinity here.

She was whispering: "It was - was poor George whom Miko shot."

I had now the true version of what had occurred. Miko had been forcing his wooing upon Anita. George Prince was a weakling whose only good quality was his love for his sister. Some years ago he had fallen into evil ways. Been arrested, and then been discharged from his position with the Federated Corporation. He had taken up with evil companions in Greater New York. Mostly Martians. And Miko had met him. His technical knowledge, his training with the Federated Corporation, made him valuable to Miko's enterprise. And so Prince had joined the brigands.

Of all this, Anita had been unaware. She had never liked Miko. Feared him. But it seemed that the Martian had some hold upon her brother, which puzzled and frightened Anita.

Then Miko had fallen in love with her. George had not liked it. And that night on the *Planetara*, Miko had come and knocked upon Anita's door, and incautiously she had opened it. He forced himself in. And when she repulsed him, struggled with him, George had been awakened.

She was whispering to me now. "My room was dark. We were all three struggling. George was holding me - the shot came - and I screamed."

And Miko had fled, not knowing whom his shot had hit in the darkness.

"And when George died, Captain Carter wanted me to

impersonate him. We planned it with Dr. Frank to try and learn what Miko and the others were doing; because I didn't know that poor George had fallen into such evil ways."

She whispered, "But I love you, Gregg. I want to be the first to say it: I love you - I love you."

We had the sanity to try and plan.

"Anita, tell Miko we discussed the multiple powers of the catalyst. Discussed how carefully it would have to be transported; how to gauge its worth. You'll have to be careful, clever. Don't say too much. Tell him we estimate the value at about a hundred and thirty millions."

I repeated what Miko had told me of his plans. She knew all that. And Snap knew it. She had a few moments alone with Snap and gave me now a message from him, "We'll pull out of this, Gregg."

With Snap she had worked out a plan. There were Snap and I; and Shac and Dud Ardley upon whom we could doubtless depend. And Dr. Frank. Against us were Miko and his sister, and Coniston and Hahn. Of course, there were the members of the crew. But we were numerically the stronger when it came to true leadership. Unarmed and guarded now. But if we could break loose - recapture the ship....

I sat listening to Anita's eager whispers. It seemed feasible. Miko did not altogether trust George Prince; Anita was now unarmed.

"But I can make opportunity! I can get one of their ray cylinders, and an invisible cloak equipment."

That cloak, that had been hidden in Miko's room when Carter searched for it in A20 was now in the chart room by Johnson's body. It had been repaired now. Anita thought she could get possession of it.

We worked out the details of the plan. Anita would arm herself, and come and release me. Together, with a paralyzing ray, we could creep about the ship, overcome these brigands, one by one. There were so few of the leaders. With them felled, and with us in control of the turret and the radio room, we could force the crew to stay at their posts. There were, Anita said, no navigators among Miko's crew. They would not dare oppose us.

"But it should be done at once, Anita. In a few hours we will be at the asteroid."

"Yes. I will go now and try to get the weapons."

"Where is Snap?"

"Still in the radio room. One of the crew guards him."

Coniston was roaming the ship. He was still loitering on the deck, watching my door. Hahn was in the turret. The morning watch of the crew were at their posts in the hull corridors. The stewards were preparing a morning meal. There were nine members of subordinates altogether, Anita had calculated. Six of them were in Miko's pay. The other three - our own men who had not been killed in the fighting - had joined the brigands.

"And Dr. Frank, Anita?"

He was in the lounge. All the passengers were herded there, with Miko and Moa alternating on guard.

"I will arrange it with Venza," Anita whispered swiftly. "She will tell the others. Dr. Frank knows about it now. He thinks it can be done."

The possibility of it swept me anew. The brigands were of necessity scattered singly about the ship. One by one, creeping under cover of an invisible cloak, I could fell them, and replace them without alarming others. My thoughts leaped to it. We would strike down the guard in the radio room. Release Snap. At the turret we could assail Hahn, and replace him with Snap.

Coniston's voice outside broke in upon us. "Prince."

He was coming forward. Anita stood in the doorway. "I have the figures, Coniston. By God, this Haljan is with us! And clever! We think it will total a hundred and thirty millions. What a stake!"

She whispered, "Gregg dear, I'll be back soon. We can do it – be ready!"

"Anita - be careful of yourself! If they should suspect you...."

"I'll be careful. In an hour, Gregg, or less, I'll come back.... All right, Coniston. Where is Miko? I want to see him. Stay where you are, Haljan. In good time Miko will trust you with your liberty. You'll be rich like all of us. Never fear."

She swaggered out upon the deck, waved at the brigand, and banged my cubby door in my face.

I sat upon my bunk. Waiting. Would she come back? Would she be successful?

XVI

She came. I suppose it was no more than an hour: It seemed an eternity of apprehension. There was the slight hissing of the seal of my door. The panel slid. I had leaped from my bunk where in the darkness I was lying tense.

"Prince?" I did not dare say "Anita."

"Gregg."

Her voice. My gaze swept the deck as the panel opened. Neither Coniston nor anyone else was in sight, save Anita's dark-robed figure which came into my room.

"You got it?" I asked in a low whisper.

I held her for an instant, kissed her. But she pushed me away with quick hands. She was breathless.

"Yes, I have it. Give us a little light - we must hurry!"

In the blue dimness I saw that she was holding one of the Martian cylinders. The smaller size: it would paralyze but not kill.

"Only one, Anita?"

"Yes. And this -"

The invisible cloak. We laid it on my grid, and I adjusted its mechanism. I donned it and drew its hood, and threw on its current.

"All right, Anita?"

"Yes."

"Can you see me?"

"No." She had stepped back a foot or two. "Not from here. But you must let no one approach too close."

Then she came forward, put out her hand, fumbled until she found me.

It was our plan to have me follow her out. Anyone observing us would see only the robed figure of the supposed George Prince, and I would escape unnoticed.

The situation about the ship was almost unchanged. Anita had secured the weapon and the cloak and slipped away to my cubby without being observed.

"You're sure of that?"

"I think so, Gregg. I was careful."

Moa was now in the lounge, guarding the passengers. Hahn was asleep in the chart room. Coniston was in the turret. Coniston would be off duty presently, Anita said, with Hahn taking his place. There were lookouts in the forward and stern watch towers, and a guard upon Snap in the radio room.

"Is he inside the room, Anita?"

"Snap? Yes."

"No - the guard."

"The guard was sitting on the spider bridge at the door."

This was unfortunate. That guard could see all the deck clearly. He might be suspicious of George Prince wandering around: it would be difficult to get near enough to assail him. This cylinder, I knew, had an effective range of only some twenty feet.

"Coniston is the sharpest, Gregg. He will be the hardest to get near."

"Where is Miko?"

The brigand leader had gone below a few moments ago, down into the hull corridor. Anita had seized the opportunity to come to me.

"We can attack Hahn in the chart room first," I whispered. "And get the other weapons. Are they still there?"

"Yes. But the forward deck is very bright, Gregg."

We were approaching the asteroid. Already its light, like a brilliant moon, was brightening the forward deck space. It made me realize how much haste was necessary.

We decided to go down into the hull corridors. Locate Miko. Fell him and hide him. His nonappearance back on deck would very soon throw the others into confusion, especially now with our impending landing upon the asteroid. And, under cover of this confusion, we would try to release Snap.

We were ready. Anita slid my door open. She stepped through, with me soundlessly scurrying after her. The empty, silent deck was alternately dark with shadow patches and bright with blobs of starlight. A sheen of the Sun's corona was mingled with it; and from forward came the radiance of the asteroid's mellow silver glow.

Anita turned to seal my door; within my faintly humming cloak I stood beside her. Was I invisible in this light? Almost directly over us, close under the dome, the lookout sat in his little tower. He gazed down at Anita.

Amidships, high over the cabin superstructure, the radio room hung dark and silent. The guard on its bridge was visible. He too, looked down.

A tense instant. Then I breathed again. There was no alarm. The two guards answered Anita's gesture.

Anita said aloud into my empty cubby: "Miko will come for you presently, Haljan. He told me that he wants you at the turret controls to land us on the asteroid."

She finished sealing my door and turned away; started forward along the deck. I followed. My steps were soundless in my elastic-bottomed shoes. Anita swaggered with a noisy tread. Near the door of the smoking room a small incline passage led downward. We went into it.

The passage was dimly blue lit. We descended its length, came to the main corridor, which ran the length of the hull. A vaulted metal passage, with doors to the control rooms opening from it. Dim lights showed at intervals.

The humming of the ship was more apparent here. It drowned the light humming of my cloak. I crept after Anita; my hand under the cloak clutched the ray weapon.

A steward passed us. I shrank aside to avoid him.

Anita spoke to him. "Where is Miko, Ellis?"

"In the ventilator room, Miss. Prince. There was difficulty with the air renewal."

Anita nodded and moved on. I could have felled that steward

as he passed me. Oh, if I only had, how different things might have been!

But it seemed needless. I let him go, and he turned into a nearby door which led to the galley.

Anita moved forward. If we could come upon Miko alone! Abruptly she turned and whispered, "Gregg, if other men are with him, I'll draw him away. You watch your chance."

What little things can overthrow one's careful plans! Anita had not realized how close to her I was following. And her turning so unexpectedly caused me to collide with her sharply.

"Oh!" She exclaimed it involuntarily. Her outflung hand had unwittingly gripped my wrist, caught the electrode there. The touch burned her, and short-circuited my robe. There was a hiss. My current burned out the tiny fuses.

My invisibility was gone! I stood, a tall, blackhooded figure, revealed to the gaze of anyone who might be near!

The futile plans of humans! We had planned so carefully! Our calculations, our hopes of what we could do, came clattering now in a sudden wreckage around us.

"Anita! Run!"

If I were seen with her, then her own disguise would probably be discovered. That above everything, would be disaster.

"Anita, get away from me! I must try it alone!"

I could hide somewhere, repair the cloak perhaps. Or, since now I was armed, why could not I boldly start an assault?

"Gregg, we must get you back to your cubby!" She was clinging to me in panic.

"No. You run! Get away from me! Don't you understand? George Prince has no business here with me! They'll kill you!"

"Gregg, let's get back to the deck."

I pushed at her, both of us in confusion.

From behind me there came a shout. That accursed steward! He had returned, to investigate perhaps what George Prince was doing in this corridor. He heard our voices. His shout in the silence of the ship sounded horribly loud. The white-cloaked shape of him was in the nearby doorway. He stood stricken with surprise at seeing me. And then turned to run.

I fired my paralyzing cylinder through my cloak. Got him! He fell. I shoved Anita violently.

"Run! Tell Miko to come - tell him you heard a shout. He won't suspect you!"

"But, Gregg -"

"You mustn't be found out. You're our only hope, Anita! I'll hide, fix the cloak, or get back to my cubby. We'll try again."

It decided her. She scurried down the corridor. I whirled the other way. The steward's shout might not have been heard.

Then realization flashed to me. That steward would be revived. He was one of Miko's men. He would be revived and tell what he had seen and heard. Anita's disguise would be revealed.

A cold-blooded killing, I do protest, went against me. But it was necessary. I flung myself upon him. I beat his skull with the metal of my cylinder.

I stood up. My hood had fallen back from my head. I wiped my bloody hands on my useless cloak. I had smashed the cylinder.

"Haljan!"

Anita's voice! A sharp note of horror and warning. I became aware that in the corridor, forty feet down its dim length, Miko had appeared with Anita behind him. His bullet projector was leveled. It spat at me. But Anita had pulled at his arm.

The explosive report was sharply deafening in the confined space of the corridor. With a spurt of flame the leaden pellet struck over my head against the vaulted ceiling.

Miko was struggling with Anita. "Prince, you idiot!"

"Miko, it's Haljan! Don't kill him -"

The turmoil brought members of the crew. From the shadowed oval near me they came running. I flung the useless cylinder at them. But I was trapped in the narrow passage.

I might have fought my way out. Or Miko might have shot me. But there was the danger that, in her horror, Anita would betray herself.

I backed against the wall. "Don't kill me! See, I will not fight!"

I flung up my arms. And the crew, emboldened and courageous under Miko's gaze, leaped on me and bore me down.

The futile plans of humans! Anita and I had planned so carefully. And in a few brief minutes of action it had come only to this!

XVII

"So, Gregg Haljan, you are not as loyal as you pretend!"

Miko was livid with suppressed anger. They had stripped the cloak from me, and flung me back in my cubby. Miko was now confronting me: at the door Moa stood watching. And Anita was behind her. I sat outwardly defiant and sullen on my bunk. But I was tense and alert, fearful still of what Anita's emotion might betray her into doing.

"Not so loyal," Miko repeated. "And a fool!"

"How did he get out of here? Prince, you came in here!"

My heart was wildly thumping. But Anita retorted with a touch of spirit, "I came to tell him what you commanded. To check Hahn's latest figures - and to be ready to take the controls when we approached the asteroid."

"Well, how did he get out?"

"How should I know?" she parried. Little actress! Her spirit helped to allay my fear. She held her cloak close around her in the fashion they had come to expect from the George Prince who had just buried his sister. "How should I know, Miko? I sealed his door."

"But did you?"

"Of course he did," Moa put in.

"Ask your lookouts," Anita said. "They saw me - I waved to them just as I sealed the door."

I ventured, "I have been taught to open doors." I managed a sly, lugubrious smile. "I shall not try it again, Miko."

Nothing had been said about my killing of the steward. I thanked my constellations now that he was dead. "I shall not try it again," I repeated.

A glance passed between Miko and his sister. Miko said abruptly, "You seem to realize it is not my purpose to kill you. And you presume upon it."

"I shall not again." I eyed Moa. She was gazing at me steadily. She said, "Leave me with him, Miko...." She smiled. "Gregg Haljan, we are no more than twenty thousand miles from the asteroid now. The calculations for retarding are now in operation."

It was what had taken Miko below, that and trouble with the ventilating system, which was soon rectified. But the retarding of the ship's velocity when nearing a destination required accurate manipulation. These brigands were fearful of their own skill. That was obvious. It gave me confidence. I was really needed. They would not harm me. Except for Miko's impulsive temper, I was in no danger from them - not now, certainly.

Moa was saying, "I think I may make you understand, Gregg. We have tremendous riches within our grasp."

"I know it," I said with sudden thought. "But there are many with whom to divide this treasure...."

Miko caught my intended implication. "By the infernal, this fellow may have thought he could seize this treasure for himself! Because he is a navigator!"

Moa said vehemently, "Do not be an idiot, Gregg! You could not do it! There will be fighting with Grantline!"

My purpose was accomplished. They seemed to see me a willing outlaw like themselves. As though it were a bond between us.

"Leave me with him," said Moa.

Miko acquiesced. "For a few minutes only." He proffered a heat ray cylinder but she refused it.

"I am not afraid of him."

Miko swung on me. "Within an hour we will be nearing the atmosphere. Will you take the controls?"

"Yes."

He set his heavy jaw. His eyes bored into me. "You're a strange fellow, Haljan. I can't make you out. I am not angry now. Do you think, when I am deadly serious, that I mean what I say?"

His calm words set a sudden chill over me. I checked my smile.

"Yes," I said.

"Well then, I will tell you this: not for all of Prince's well-meaning interference, or Moa's liking for you, or my own need of your skill, will I tolerate more trouble from you. The next time, I will kill you. Do you believe me?"

"Yes."

"That is all I want to say. You kill my men, and my sister says I must not hurt you. I am not a child to be ruled by a woman!"

He held his huge fist before my face. "With these fingers I will twist your neck! Do you believe it?"

"Yes." I did indeed.

He swung on his heel. "Moa wants to try and put sense in your head - I hope she does it. Bring him to the lounge when you have finished. Come, Prince, Hahn will need us." He chuckled grimly. "Hahn seems to fear we will plunge into this asteroid like a wild comet gone suddenly tangent!"

Anita moved aside to let him through the door. I caught a glimpse of her set white face as she followed him down the deck. Then Moa's bulk blocked the doorway. She faced me.

"Sit where you are, Gregg." She turned and closed the door upon us. "I am not afraid of you. Should I be?"

"No."

She came and sat down beside me. "If you should attempt to leave this room, the stern lookout has orders to bore you through."

"I have no intention of leaving this room," I retorted. "I do not want to commit suicide."

"I thought you did. You seem minded in such a fashion. Gregg, why are you so heedless?"

I said carefully, "This treasure - you are many who will divide it. You have all these men on the *Planetara*. And in Ferrok-Shahn, others -"

I paused. Would she tell me? Could I make her talk of that other brigand ship which Miko had said was waiting on Mars? I wondered if he had been able to signal it. The distance from here to Mars was great; yet upon other voyages Snap's signals had gotten through. My heart sank at the thought. Our situation here was desperate enough. The passengers soon would be cast upon the asteroid: there would be left only Snap, Anita and myself. We might recapture the ship, but I doubted it now. My thoughts were turning to our arrival on the Moon. We three might, perhaps, be able to thwart the attack upon Grantline, hold the brigands off until help from the Earth might come.

But with another brigand ship, fully manned and armed, coming from Mars, the condition would be immeasurably worse. Grantline had some twenty men, and his camp, I knew, would be reasonably fortified. I knew too, that Johnny Grantline would fight to his last man.

Moa was saying, "I would like to tell you our plans, Gregg."

Her gaze was on my face. Keen eyes, but they were luminous now - an emotion in them sweeping her. But outwardly she was calm.

"Well, why don't you tell me?" I said. "If I am to help...."

"Gregg, I want you with us. Don't you understand. And we are not many, really. My brother and I are guiding this affair. With your help, I would feel differently."

"The ship at Ferrok-Shahn -"

My fears were realized. She said, "I think our signals reached it. Dean tried and Coniston was checking him."

"You think the ship is coming?"

"Yes."

"Where will it join us?"

"At the Moon. We will be there in thirty hours. Your figures gave that, did they not?"

"Yes," I said. "And the other ship - how fast is it?"

"Quite fast. In eight days - perhaps nine, it will reach the Moon."

She seemed willing enough to talk. There was indeed, no reason why she shouldn't: I could not, she naturally felt, turn the knowledge to account. Certainly my position seemed desperately helpless.

"Manned -" I prompted.

"About forty men."

"And armed? Long range projectors?"

"You ask very avid questions, Gregg!"

"Why should I not? Don't you suppose I'm interested?" I touched her. "Moa, did it ever occur to you, if once you and Miko trusted me - which you don't - I might show more interest in joining you?"

The look on her face emboldened me. "Did you ever think of that, Moa? And some arrangement for my share of this treasure? I am not like Johnson, to be hired for a hundred pounds of gold leaf."

"Gregg, I will see that you get your share. Riches for you and me."

"I was thinking, Moa - when we land at the Moon tomorrow - where is our equipment?"

The Moon, with its lack of atmosphere, needed special equipment. I had never heard Captain Carter mention what apparatus the *Planetara* was carrying.

Moa laughed. "We have located air suits and helmets - a

variety of suitable apparatus, Gregg. But we were not foolish enough to leave Greater New York on this voyage without our own apparatus. My brother and Coniston and Prince - all of us snipped crates of freight consigned to Ferrok-Shahn; and Rankin had special baggage marked 'theatrical apparatus.'"

I understood it now. These brigands had boarded the *Planetara* with their own Moon equipment, disguised as freight and personal baggage. Shipped in bond, to be inspected by the tax officials of Mars.

"It is on board now. We will open it when we leave the asteroid, Gregg. We are well equipped."

She bent toward me. And suddenly her long, lean fingers were gripping my shoulders.

"Gregg, look at me!"

I gazed into her eyes. There was passion there; and her voice was intense.

"Gregg, I told you once a Martian girl goes after what she wants. It is you I want -"

Not for me to play upon a woman's emotions! "Moa, you flatter me."

"I love you." She held me off, gazing at me. "Gregg -"

I must have smiled. Abruptly she released me.

"So you think it amusing?"

"No. But on Earth -"

"We are not on Earth. Nor am I of the Earth!" She was gauging me keenly. No note of pleading was in her voice: a stern authority, and the passion was swinging to anger.

"I am like my brother: I do not understand you, Gregg Haljan. Perhaps you think you are clever?"

"Perhaps."

There was a moment of silence. "Gregg, I said I loved you. Have you no answer?"

"No." In truth, I did not know what sort of answer it would be best to make. Whatever she must have read in my eyes, it stirred her to fury. Her fingers with the strength of a man in them, dug into my shoulders. Her gaze searched me.

"You think you love someone else? Is that it?"

That was horribly startling; but she did not mean it just that way. She amended, with caustic venom: "That little Anita Prince! You thought you loved her! Was that it?"

"No!"

But I hardly deceived her. "Sacred to her memory! Her ratlike little face, soft voice like a purring, sniveling cat! Is that what you're remembering, Gregg Haljan?"

I tried to laugh. "What nonsense!"

"Is it? Then why are you cold under my touch? Am I, a girl descended from the Martian flame-workers, impotent to awaken a man?"

A woman scorned! In all the universe there could be no more dangerous an enemy. An incredible venom shot from her eyes.

"That miserable mouselike creature! Well for her that my brother killed her."

It struck me cold. If Anita were unmasked, beyond all the menace of Miko's wooing, I knew that the venom of Moa's jealousy was a greater danger.

I said sharply, "Don't be simple, Moa!" I shook off her grip. "You imagine too much. You forget that I am a man of Earth and you a girl of Mars."

"Is that reason why we should not love?"

"No. But our instincts are different. Men of Earth are born to the chase."

I was smiling. With thought of Anita's danger I could find it readily in my heart to dupe this Amazon.

"Give me time, Moa. You attract me."

"You lie!"

"Do you think so?" I gripped her arm with all the power of my fingers. It must have hurt her but she gave no sign; her gaze clung to me steadily.

"I don't know what to think, Gregg Haljan...."

I held my grip. "Think what you like. Men of Earth have been known to kill the thing they love."

"You want me to fear you?"

"Perhaps."

She smiled scornfully. "That is absurd."

I released her. I said earnestly, "I want you to realize that if you treat me fairly, I can be of great advantage to this venture. There will be fighting. I am fearless."

Her venomous expression was softening. "I think that is true, Gregg!"

"And you need my navigating skill. Even now I should be in the turret."

I stood up. I half expected she would stop me, but she did not. I added, "Shall we go?"

She stood beside me. Her height brought her face level with mine.

"I think you will cause no more trouble, Gregg?"

"Of course not. I am not wholly witless."

"You have been."

"Well, that is over." I hesitated. Then I added, "A man of Earth does not yield to love while there is work to do. This treasure -"

I think that of everything I said, this last most convinced her.

She interrupted, "That I understand." Her eyes were smoldering. "When it is over - when we are rich - then I will claim you, Gregg."

She turned from me. "Are you ready?"

"Yes. No! I must get that sheet of Hahn's last figures."

"Are they checked?"

"Yes." I picked the sheet up from my desk. "Hahn is fairly accurate, Moa."

"A fool, nevertheless. An apprehensive fool."

A comradeship seemed coming between us. It was my purpose to establish it.

"Are we going to maroon Dr. Frank with the passengers?" I asked.

"Yes."

"But he may be of use to us."

Moa shook her head decisively. "My brother has decided not. We will be well rid of Dr. Frank. Are you ready, Gregg?"

"Yes."

She opened the door. Her gesture reassured the lookout, who was alertly watching the stern watchtower.

I stepped out, and followed her forward along the deck, which now was bright with the radiance of the nearby asteroid.

XVIII

A fair little world. I had thought so before; and I thought so now as I gazed at the asteroid hanging so close before our bow. A huge, thin crescent, with the Sun off to one side behind it. A silver crescent, tinged with red. From this near vantage point, all of the little globe's disc was visible. The seas lay in gray patches. The convexity of the disc was sharply defined. So small a world! Fair and beautiful, shrouded with clouded areas.

"Where is Miko?"

"In the lounge, Gregg?"

"Can we stop there?"

Moa turned into the lounge archway. Strange, tense scene. I saw Anita at once. Her robed figure lurked in an inconspicuous corner; her eyes were upon me as Moa and I entered, but she did not move. The thirty-odd passengers were huddled in a group. Solemn, white-faced men; frightened women. Some of them were sobbing. One Earth woman - a young widow - sat holding her little girl, and wailing with uncontrolled hysteria. The child knew me. As I appeared now, with my gold laced white coat over my shoulders, the little girl seemed to see in my uniform a mark of authority. She left her mother and ran to me.

"You - please, will you help us? My Moms is crying."

I sent her gently back. But there came upon me then a compassion for these innocent passengers, fated to have embarked on this ill-fated voyage. Herded here in this cabin, with brigands like pirates of old, guarding them. Waiting now to be marooned on an uninhabited asteroid roaming in space. A sense of responsibility swept me. I swung upon Miko. He stood with a nonchalant grace, lounging against the wall with a cylinder dangling in his hand. He anticipated me, and was the first to speak.

"So, Haljan, she put some sense into your head? No more trouble? Then get into the turret. Moa, stay there with him. Send Hahn here. Where is that ass, Coniston? We will be in the atmosphere shortly."

I said, "No more trouble from me, Miko. But these passengers - what preparation are you making for them on the asteroid?"

He stared in surprise. Then he laughed. "I am no murderer. The crew is preparing food, all we can spare. And tools. They can build themselves shelter - they will be picked up in a few weeks."

Dr. Frank was here. I caught his gaze but he did not speak. On the lounge couches there still lay the five bodies. Rankin, who had been killed by Blackstone in the fight; a man passenger killed; a woman and a man wounded, as well.

Miko added, "Dr. Frank will take his medical supplies and will care for the wounded. There are other bodies among the crew." His gesture was deprecating. "I have not buried them. We will put them ashore; easier that way."

The passengers were all eying me. I said:

"You have nothing to fear. I will guarantee you the best equipment we can spare." I turned to Miko. "You will give them apparatus with which to signal?"

"Yes. Get to the turret."

I turned away, with Moa after me. Again the little girl ran forward.

"Come ... speak to my Moms; she is crying."

It was across the cabin from Miko. Coniston had appeared from the deck; it created a slight diversion. He joined Miko.

"Wait," I said to Moa. "She is afraid of you. This is humanity."

I pushed Moa back. I followed the child. I had seen that Venza was sitting with the child's weeping mother. This was a ruse to get a word with me.

I stood before the terrified woman while the child clung to my legs.

I said gently, "Don't be so frightened. Dr. Frank will take care of you. There is no danger; you will be safer on the asteroid than here on the ship." I leaned down and touched her shoulder. "There is no danger."

I was between Venza and the open cabin. Venza whispered swiftly, "When we are landing, Gregg, I want you to make a commotion - anything - just as the women go ashore."

"Why? Of course you will have food, Mrs. Francis."

"Never mind details! An instant - just confusion. Go, Gregg - don't speak now!"

I raised the child. "You take care of Mother." I kissed her.

From across the cabin, Miko's sardonic voice made me turn. "Touching sentimentality, Haljan! Get to your post in the turret!"

His rasping note of annoyance brooked no delay. I set the child down. I said, "I will land us in an hour. Depend on it."

Hahn was at the controls when Moa and I reached the turret.

"You will land us safely, Haljan?" he demanded anxiously.

I pushed him away. "Miko wants you in the lounge."

"You take command here?"

"Yes. I am no more anxious for a crash than you are, Hahn."

He sighed with relief. "That is true, of course. I am no expert at atmospheric entry."

"Have no fear. Sit down, Moa."

I waved to the lookout in the forward watch tower, and got his routine gesture. I rang the corridor bells, and the normal signals came promptly back.

I turned to Hahn. "Get along, won't you? Tell Miko that things are all right here."

Hahn's small dark figure, lithe as a leopard in his tight fitting trousers and jacket with his robe now discarded, went swiftly down the spider incline and across the deck.

"Moa, where is Snap? By the infernal - if he has been injured -"

Up on the radio room bridge, the brigand guard still sat. Then I saw that Snap was out there sitting with him. I waved from the turret window, and Snap's cheery gesture answered me. His voice carried down through the silver moonlight: "Land us safely, Gregg. These weird amateur navigators!"

Within the hour I had us dropping into the asteroid's atmosphere. The ship heated steadily. The pressure went up. It kept me busy with the instruments and the calculations. But my signals were always promptly answered from below. The brigand crew did its part efficiently.

At a hundred and fifty thousand feet I shifted the gravity plates to the landing combinations, and started the electronic engines.

"All safe, Gregg?" Moa sat at my elbow; her eyes, with what seem a glow of admiration in them, followed my busy routine activities.

"Yes. The crew works well."

The electronic streams flowed out like a rocket tail behind us. The *Planetara* caught their impetus. In the rarefied air, our bow lifted slightly, like a ship riding a gentle ground swell. At a hundred thousand feet we sailed gently forward, hull down to the asteroid's surface, cruising to seek a landing space.

A little sea was now beneath us. A shadowed sea, deep purple in the night down there. Occasional verdurous islands showed, with the lines of white surf marking them. Beyond the sea, a curving coastline was visible. Rocky headlines, behind which mountain foothills rose in serrated, verdurous ranks. The sunlight edged the distant mountains; and presently this rapidly turning little world brought the sunlight forward.

It was day beneath us. We slid gently downward. Thirty thousand feet now, above a sparkling blue ocean. The coastline was just ahead; green with a lush, tropical vegetation. Giant trees, huge-leaved. Long, dangling vines; air plants, with giant pods and vivid orchidlike blossoms.

I sat at the turret window, staring through my glasses. A fair, little world, yet obviously uninhabited. I could fancy that all this was newly sprung vegetation. This asteroid had whirled in from the cold of the interplanetary space, far outside our solar system. A few years ago - as time might be measured astronomically, it was no more than yesterday - this fair landscape was congealed white and bleak with a sweep of glacial ice. But the seeds of life miraculously were here. The miracle of life! Under the warming, germinating sunlight, the verdure had sprung.

"Can you find landing space, Gregg?" Moa's question brought back my wandering fancies. I saw an upland glade, a level spread of ferns with the forest banked around it. A cliff height nearby, frowning down at the sea.

"Yes. I can land us there." I showed her through the glasses. I rang the sirens, and we spiraled, descending further. The mountain tops were now close beneath us. Clouds were overhead, white masses with blue sky behind them. A day of brilliant sunlight. But soon, with our forward cruising, it was night. The sunlight dropped beneath the sharply convex horizon; the sea and the land went purple.

A night of brilliant stars; the Earth was a blazing blue-red point of light. The heavens visibly were revolving; in an hour or so it would be daylight again.

On the forward deck now Coniston had appeared, commanding half a dozen of the crew. They were carrying up caskets of food and the equipment which was to be given the marooned passengers. And making ready the disembarking incline, loosening the seals of the side dome windows.

Sternward on the deck, by the lounge oval, I could see Miko standing. And occasionally the roar of his voice at the passengers, sounded.

My vagrant thoughts flung back into Earth's history. Like this, ancient travelers of the surface of the sea were herded by pirates to walk the plank, or be put ashore, marooned upon some fair desert island of the tropic Spanish main.

Hahn came mounting our turret incline. "All is well,

Gregg Haljan?"

"Get to your work," Moa told him sharply.

He retreated, joining the bustle and confusion which now was beginning on the deck. It struck me - could I turn that confusion to account? Would it be possible, now at the last moment, to attack these brigands? Snap still sat outside the radio room doorway. But his guard was alert with upraised projector. And that guard, I saw, in his position, commanded all the deck.

And I saw too, as the passengers now were herded in a line from the lounge oval, that Miko had roped and bound all of the men, a clanking chain connected them. They came like a line of convicts, marching forward, and stopped on the open deck near the base of the turret. Dr. Frank's grim face gazed up at me.

Miko ordered the women and children in a group beside the chained men. His words to them reached me: "You are in no danger. When we land, be careful. You will find gravity very different - this is a very small world."

I flung on the landing lights; the deck glowed with the blue radiance; the searchbeams shot down beside our hull. We hung now a thousand feet above the forest glade. I cut off the electronic streams. We poised, with the gravity plates set at normal, and only a gentle night breeze to give us a slight side drift. This I could control with the lateral propeller rudders.

For all my busy landing routine, my mind was on other things. Venza's swift words back there in the lounge. I was to create a commotion while the passengers were landing. Why? Had she and Dr. Frank some last minute desperate purposes?

I determined I would do what she said. Shout, or mis-order the lights. That would be easy.

I was glad it was night. I had, indeed, calculated our descent so that the landing would be in darkness. But to what purpose? These brigands were very alert. There was nothing I could think of to do which would avail us anything more than a probable swift death under Miko's anger.

"Well done, Gregg!" said Moa.

I cut off the last of the propellers. With scarcely a perceptible jar, the *Planetara* grounded, rose like a feather, and settled to rest in the glade. The deep purple night with stars overhead was around us. I hissed out our interior air through the dome and hull ports, and admitted the night air of the asteroid. My calculations - of necessity mere mathematical approximations - proved fairly accurate. In temperature and pressure there was no radical change as the dome windows slid back.

We had landed. Whatever Venza's purpose, her moment was at hand. I was tense. But I was aware also, that beside me Moa was very alert. I had thought her unarmed. She was not. She sat back from me; in her hand was a long thin knife blade.

She murmured tensely, "You have done your part, Gregg. Well and skillfully done. Now we will sit here quietly and watch them land."

Snap's guard was standing, keenly watching. The lookouts in the forward and stern towers were also armed; I could see them both gazing keenly down at the confusion of the blue lit deck.

The incline went over the hull side and touched the ground.

"Enough!" Miko roared. "The men first. Hahn, move the women back! Coniston, pile those caskets to the side. Get out of the way, Prince."

Anita was down there. I saw her at the edge of the group of women. Venza was near her.

Miko shoved her. "Get out of the way, Prince. You can help Coniston. Have the things ready to throw off."

Five of the steward crew were at the head of the incline. Miko shouted up at me:

"Haljan, hold our shipboard gravity normal."

"Yes."

The line of men were first to descend. Dr. Frank led them. He flashed a look of farewell up at me and Snap as he went down the incline with the chained men passengers after him.

Motley procession! Twenty odd, disheveled, half-clothed men of these worlds. The changing, lightening gravity on the incline caught them. Dr. Frank bounded up to the rail under the impetus of his step; caught and held himself. Drew himself back. The line swayed. In the dim, blue lit glare it seemed unreal, crazy. A grotesque dream of men descending a plank.

They reached the forest glade. Stood swaying, afraid at first to move. The purple night crowded them; they stood gazing at this strange world, their new prison.

"Now the women."

Miko was shoving the women to the head of the incline. I could feel Moa's gaze upon me. Her knife gleamed in the turret light.

She murmured again, "In a few moments you can bring us away, Gregg."

I felt like an actor awaiting his cue in the wings of some turgid drama the plot of which he did not know. Venza was near the head of the incline. Some of the women and children were on it. A woman screamed. Her child had slipped from her hand; bounded up over the rail and fallen. Hardly fallen - floated down to the ground, with flailing arms and legs, landing in the dark ferns unharmed. Its terrified wail came up.

There was a confusion on the incline. Venza, still on the deck, seemed to send a look of appeal to the turret. My cue?

I slid my hand to the light switchboard. It was near my knees. I pulled a switch. The blue lit deck beneath the turret went dark.

I recall an instant of horrible, tense silence, and in the gloom beside me I was aware of Moa moving. I felt a thrill of instinctive fear - would she plunge that knife into me?

The silence of the darkened deck was broken with a confusion of sounds. A babble of voices; a woman passenger's scream; shuffling feet; and above it all, Miko's roar:

"Stand quiet! Everyone! No movement!"

On the descending incline there was chaos. The disembarking women were clinging to the gang rail; some of them had evidently surged forward and fallen. Down on the ground in the purple-shadowed starlight, I could vaguely see the chained line of men. They too, were in confusion, trying to shove themselves toward the fallen women.

Miko roared: "Light those tubes! Gregg Haljan! By the Almighty, Moa, are you up there? What is wrong? The light tubes -"

Dark drama of unknown plot! I wondered if I should try and leave the turret. Where was Anita? She had been down there on the deck when I flung out the lights.

I think twenty seconds would have covered it all. I had not moved. I thought, "Is Snap concerned with this?"

Moa's knife could have stabbed me. I felt her lunge against me.

And suddenly I was gripping her, twisting her wrist. But she flung the knife away. Her strength was almost the equal of my own. Her hand went for my throat, and with the other hand she was fumbling.

The deck abruptly sprang into light again. Moa had found the switch and threw it back.

She fought me as I tried to reach the switch. I saw down on the deck. Miko was gazing up at us. Moa panted, "Gregg - stop! If he sees you doing this, he'll kill you."

The scene down there was almost unchanged. I had answered my cue. To what purpose? I saw Anita near Miko. The last of the women were on the plank.

I had stopped struggling with Moa. She sat back, panting. And then she called:

"Sorry, Miko. It will not happen again."

Miko was in a towering rage. But he was too busy to bother with me; his anger swung on those nearest him. He shoved the last of the women violently at the incline. She bounded over. Her body, with the gravity pull of only a few Earth pounds, sailed in an arc and dropped near the swaying line of men.

Miko swung back. "Get out of my way!" A sweep of his huge arm knocked Anita sidewise. "Prince, damn you, help me with those boxes!"

The frightened stewards were lifting the boxes, square metal storage chests each as long as a man, packed with food, tools, and equipment.

"Here, get out of my way! All of you!"

My breath came again; Anita nimbly retreated before Miko's angry rush. He dashed at the stewards. Three of them held a box. He took it from them; raised it at the top of the incline, poised it over his head an instant, with his massive arms like gray pillars beneath it; and flung it. The box catapulted, dropped; and then passing the *Planetara's* gravity area, it sailed in a long flat arc over the forest glade and crashed into the purple underbrush.

"Give me another!"

The stewards pushed another at him. Like an angry Titan, he flung it. And another. One by one the chests sailed out and crashed.

"There is your food. Go pick it up! Haljan, make ready to ring us away!"

On the deck lay the dead body of Rance Rankin, which the stewards had carried out. Miko seized it: flung it.

"There! Go to your last resting place!"

And the other bodies, Balch, Blackstone, Captain Carter, Johnson - Miko flung them all. And the course masters and those of our crew who had been killed.

The passengers were all on the ground now. It was dim down there. I tried to distinguish Venza, but could not. I could see Dr. Frank's figure at the end of the chained line of men. The passengers were gazing in horror at the bodies hurtling over them.

"Ready, Haljan?"

Moa prompted me. "Tell him yes!"

I called, "Yes!" Had Venza failed in her unknown purpose? It seemed so. On the radio room bridge Snap and his guard stood like silent statues in the blue lit gloom.

The disembarkation was over.

"Close the ports!" Miko commanded.

The incline came folding up with a clatter. The port and dome windows slid closed. Moa hissed against my ear:

"If you want life, Gregg Haljan, you will start your duties!"

Venza had failed. Whatever it was, it had come to nothing. Down in the purple forest, disconnected now from the ship, the last of our friends stood marooned. I could distinguish them through the blur of the closed dome - only a swaying, huddled group was visible. But my fancy pictured this last sight of them, Dr. Frank, Venza, Shac and Dud Ardley.

They were gone. There were left only Snap, Anita and myself.

I was mechanically ringing us away. I heard my sirens sounding down below, with the answering clangs here in the turret. The *Planetara's* respiratory controls started; the pressure equalizers began operating; and the gravity plates began shifting into lifting combinations.

The ship was hissing and quivering with it, combined with the grating of the last of the dome ports. And Miko's command:

"Lift, Haljan!"

Hahn had been mingling with the confusion of the deck though I had hardly noticed him. Coniston had remained below with the crew answering my signals. Hahn stood now with Miko, gazing down through a deck window. Anita was alone at another.

"Lift, Haljan!"

I lifted up gently, bow first, with a repulsion of the bow plates. And started the central electronic engine. Its thrust from the stern moved us diagonally over the purple forest trees.

The glade slid downward and away. I caught a last vague glimpse of the huddled group of marooned passengers, staring up at us. Left to their fate, alone on this deserted world.

With the three engines going, we slid smoothly upward. The forest dropped, a purple spread of treetops edged with starlight and Earthlight. The sharply curving horizon seemed to follow us upward. I swung on all the power. We mounted at a forty degree angle, slowly circling, with a bank of clouds over us to the side and the shining little sea beneath.

"Very good, Gregg." In the turret light Moa's eyes blazed at me. "I do not know what you meant by darkening the deck lights." Her fingers dug at my shoulders. "I will tell my brother it was an error."

I said, "An error - yes."

"I didn't know what it was. But you have me to deal with now. You understand? I will tell my brother so. You said, 'On Earth a man may kill the thing he loves.' A woman of Mars may do that! Beware of me, Gregg Haljan."

Her passion-filled eyes bored into me. Love? Hate? The venom of a woman scorned - a mingling of turgid emotions....

I twisted back from her grip and ignored her. She sat back, silently watching my busy activities: the calculations of the shifting conditions of gravity, pressures, temperatures; a checking of the instruments on the board before me.

Mechanical routine. My mind went to Venza, back there on the asteroid. The wandering little world was already shrinking to a convex surface beneath us. Venza, with her last unknown play, gone to failure. Had I missed my cue? Whatever my part, it seemed now that I must have horribly misacted it.

The crescent Earth was presently swinging over our bow. We rocketed out of the asteroid's shadow. The glowing, flaming Sun appeared, making a crescent of the Earth. With the glass I could see our tiny Moon, visually seeming to hug the limb of its parent Earth.

We were on our course to the Moon. My mind flung ahead. Grantline with his treasure, unsuspecting this brigand ship. And suddenly, beyond all thought of Grantline, there came to me a fear for Anita. In God's truth I had been, so far, a very stumbling, inept champion, doomed to failure with everything I tried. Why had I not contrived to have Anita desert at the asteroid? Would it not have been far better for her there, taking her chance for rescue with Dr. Frank, Venza and the others?

But no! I had, like a fool, never thought of that! Had let her remain here on board at the mercy of these outlaws.

And I swore now, that beyond everything, I would protect her.

Futile oath! If I could have seen ahead a few hours! But I sensed the catastrophe. There was a shudder within me as I sat in that turret, docilely guiding us out through the asteroid's atmosphere, heading us upon our course for the Moon.

XIX

"Try again. By the infernal, Snap Dean, if you do anything to balk us, you die!"

Miko scanned the apparatus with keen eyes. How much technical knowledge of signaling instruments did this brigand leader have? I was tense and cold with apprehension as I sat in a corner of the radio room, watching Snap. Could Miko be fooled? Snap, I knew, was trying to fool him.

The Moon spread close beneath us. My log-chart, computed up to thirty minutes past, showed us barely some thirty thousand miles over the Moon's surface. A silver quadrant. The sunset caught the Lunar mountains, flung slanting shadows over the Lunar plains. All the disc was plainly visible. The mellow Earthlight glowed serene and pale to illumine the Lunar night.

The *Planetara* was bathed in silver. A brilliant silver glare swept the forward deck, clean white and splashed with black shadows. We had partly circled the Moon so as now to approach it from the Earthward side.

Miko for a time had been at my side in the turret. I had not seen Coniston or Hahn of recent hours. I had slept, awakened refreshed, and had a meal. Coniston and Hahn remained below, one or other of them always with the crew to execute my sirened orders. Then Coniston came to take my place in the turret, and I went with Miko to the radio room.

"You are skillful, Haljan." A measure of grim approval was in his voice. "You evidently have no wish to try and fool me in this navigation."

I had not, indeed. It is delicate work at best, coping with the intricacies of celestial mechanics upon a semicircular trajectory with retarding velocity, and with a makeshift crew we could easily have come upon real difficulty.

We hung at last, hull down, facing the Earthward hemisphere of the Lunar disc. The giant ball of the Earth lay behind and above us - the Sun over our stern quarter. With forward velocity almost checked, we poised, and Snap began his signals to the unsuspecting Grantline.

My work momentarily was over. I sat watching the radio room. Moa was here, close beside me. I felt always her watchful gaze, so that even the play of my emotions needed reining.

Miko worked with Snap. Anita too was here. To Miko and Moa it was the somber, taciturn George Prince, shrouded always in his black mourning cloak, disinclined to talk; sitting alone, brooding and sullen. This is how they thought of Anita.

Miko repeated: "By the infernal, if you try to fool me, Snap Dean!"

The small metal room, with its grid floor and low arched ceiling, glared with moonlight through its window. The moving figures of Snap and Miko were aped by the grotesque, misshapen shadows of them on the walls. Miko gigantic - a great menacing ogre. Snap small and alert - a trim, pale figure in his tight-fitting white trousers, broad-flowing belt, and white shirt open at the throat. His face was pale and drawn from lack of sleep and the torture to which Miko had subjected him earlier on the voyage. But he grinned at the brigand's words, and pushed his straggling hair closer under the red eyeshade.

The room over long periods was deadly silent, with Miko and Snap bending watchfully at the crowded banks of instruments. A silence in which my own pounding heart seemed to echo. I did not dare look at Anita, nor she at me. Snap was trying to signal Earth, not the Moon! His main grids were set in the reverse. The infra-red waves, flung from the bow window, were of a frequency which Snap and I believed that Grantline could not pick up. And over against the wall, close beside me and seemingly ignored by Snap, there was a tiny ultra-violet sender. Its faint hum and the quivering of its mirrors had so far passed unnoticed.

Would some Earth station pick it up? I prayed so. There was a thumbnail mirror here which would bring an answer.

Would some Earth telescope be able to see us? I doubted it. The pinpoint of the *Planetara's* infinitesimal bulk would be beyond vision.

Long silences, broken only by the faint hiss and murmur of Snap's instruments.

"Shall I try the graphs, Miko?"

"Yes."

I helped him with the spectro. At every level the plates showed us nothing save the scarred and pitted Moon surface. We worked for an hour. There was nothing. Bleak cold night on the Moon here beneath us. A touch of fading sunlight upon the Apennines. Up near the South Pole, Tycho with its radiating open rills stood like a grim dark maw.

Miko bent over a plate. "Something here? Is there?"

An abnormality upon the frowning ragged cliffs of Tycho? We thought so. But then it seemed not.

Another hour. No signal came from Earth. If Snap's calls were getting through we had no evidence of it. Abruptly Miko strode at me from across the room. I went cold and tense; Moa shifted, alert to my every movement. But Miko was not interested in me. A sweep of his clenched fist knocked the ultra-violet sender and its coils and mirrors in a tinkling crash to the grid at my feet.

"We don't need that, whatever it is!" He rubbed his knuckles where the violet waves had tinged them, and turned grimly back to Snap.

"Where are your ray mirrors? If the treasure lies exposed -"

This Martian's knowledge was far greater than we believed. He grinned sardonically at Anita. "If our treasure is here on this hemisphere, Prince, we should pick up its rays. Don't you think so? Or is Grantline too cautious to leave it exposed?"

Anita spoke in a careful, throaty drawl. "The rays came through enough when we passed here on the way out."

"You should know," grinned Miko. "An expert eavesdropper, Prince, I will say that for you.... Come, Dean, try something else. By God, if Grantline does not signal us, I will be likely to blame you - my patience is shortening. Shall we go closer, Haljan?"

"I don't think it would help," I said.

He nodded. "Perhaps not. Are we checked?"

"Yes." We were poised very nearly motionless. "If you wish an advance, I can ring it. But we need a surface destination now."

"True, Haljan." He stood thinking. "Would a zed-ray penetrate those crater cliffs? Tycho, for instance, at this angle?"

"It might," Snap agreed. "You think he may be on the northern inner Tycho?"

"He may be anywhere," said Miko shortly.

"If you think that," Snap persisted, "suppose we swing the *Planetara* over the South Pole. Tycho, viewed from there -"

"And take another quarter day of time?" Miko sneered. "Flash on your zed-ray; help him hook it up, Haljan."

I moved to the lens box of the spectroheliograph. It seemed that Snap was very strangely reluctant. Was it because he knew that the Grantline camp lay concealed on the north inner wall of Tycho's giant ring? I thought so. But Snap flashed a queer look at Anita. She did not see it, but I did. And I could not understand it.

My accursed, witless incapacity! If only I had taken warning!

"Here," commanded Miko. "A score of 'graphs with the zed-ray. I tell you I will comb this surface if we have to stay here until our ship comes from Ferrok-Shahn to join us!"

The Martian brigands were coming. Miko's signals had been answered. In ten days the other brigand ship, adequately manned and armed, would be here.

Snap helped me connect the zed-ray. He did not dare even to whisper to me, with Moa hovering always so close. And for all Miko's sardonic smiling, we knew that he would tolerate nothing from us now. He was fully armed and so was Moa.

I recall that several times Snap endeavored to touch me significantly. Oh, if only I had taken warning!

We finished our connecting. The dull gray point of zed-ray gleamed through the prisms to mingle with the moonlight entering the main lens. I stood with the shutter trip.

"The same interval, Snap?"

"Yes."

Beside me, I was aware of a faint reflection of the zed-ray - a gray cathedral shaft crossing the room and falling upon the opposite wall. An unreality there, as the zed-ray faintly strove to penetrate the metal room side.

I said, "Shall I make the exposure?"

Snap nodded. But that 'graph was never made. An exclamation from Moa made us all turn. The gamma mirrors were quivering! Grantline had picked our signals! With what was undoubtedly an intensified receiving equipment which Snap had not thought Grantline able to use, he had caught our faint zed-rays, which Snap was sending only to deceive Miko. And Grantline had recognized the *Planetara*, and had released his occulting screens surrounding the ore.

And upon their heels came Grantline's message. Not in the secret system he had arranged with Snap, but unsuspectingly in open code. I could read the swinging mirror, and so could Miko.

And Miko decoded it triumphantly aloud:

"Surprised but pleased your return. Approach Mid-Northern Hemisphere region of Archimedes, forty thousand off nearest Apennine range."

The message broke off. But even its importance was overshadowed. Miko stood in the center of the radio room, triumphantly reading the little indicator. Its beam swung on the scale, which chanced to be almost directly over Anita's head. I saw Miko's expression change.... A look of surprise, amazement, came over him.

"Why -"

He gasped. He stood staring. Almost stupidly staring, for an instant. And as I regarded him with fascinated horror, there came upon his heavy gray face a look of dawning comprehension. And I heard Snap's startled intake of breath. He moved to the spectro, where the zed-ray connections were still humming.

But, with a leap, Miko flung him away. "Off with you! Moa, watch him! Haljan, don't move!"

Again Miko stood staring. I saw now that he was staring at Anita!

"Why, George Prince! How strange you look!"

Anita did not move. She was stricken with horror; she shrank back against the wall, huddled in her cloak. Miko's sardonic voice came again:

"How strange you look, Prince!" He took a step forward. He was grim and calm. Horribly calm. Deliberate. Gloating like a great gray monster in human form toying with a fascinated, imprisoned bird.

"Move just a little, Prince. Let the zed-ray light fall more fully."

Anita's head was bare. That pale, Hamlet-like face. Dear God, the zed-ray light lay gray and penetrating upon it!

Miko took another step. Peering. Grinning. "How amazing, George Prince! Why, I can hardly believe it!"

Moa was armed with an electronic cylinder now. For all her amazement - what turgid emotions sweeping her I can only guess - she never took her eyes from Snap and me.

"Back! Don't move either of you!" she hissed at us.

Then Miko leaped at Anita like a giant gray leopard pouncing.

"Away with that cloak, Prince!"

I stood cold and numbed. And realization came at last. The faint zed-light had fallen by chance upon Anita's face. Penetrating the flesh; exposed, faintly glowing, the bone line of her jaw. Unmasked the art of Glutz.

Miko seized her wrists, drew her forward, beyond the shaft of zed-light, into the brilliant light of the Moon. And ripped her cloak from her. The gentle curves of her woman's figure were so unmistakable!

And as Miko gazed at them, all his calm triumph swept away.

"Why, Anita!"

I heard Moa mutter, "So that is it?" A venomous flashing look - a shaft from me to Anita and back again. "So that is it?"

"Why, Anita!"

Miko's great arms gathered her up as though she were a child. "So I have you back! From the dead, delivered back to me!"

"Gregg!" Snap's warning, and his grip on my shoulders brought me a measure of sanity. I had tensed to spring. I stood quivering, and Moa thrust her weapon against my face. The grids were swaying again with a message from Grantline. But it was ignored.

In the glare of moonlight by the forward window, Miko held Anita, his great hands pawing her with triumphant possessive caresses.

"So, little Anita, you are given back to me!"

XX

Moonlight upon Earth so gently shines to make romantic a lover's smile! But the reality of the Lunar night is cold beyond human belief. Cold and darkly silent. Grim desolation. Awesome. Majestic. A frowning majesty that even to the most intrepid human beholder is inconceivably forbidding.

And there were humans here now. On this tumbled plain, between Archimedes and the mountains, one small crater amid the million of its fellows was distinguished this night by the presence of humans. The Grantline camp! It huddled in the deepest purple shadows on the side of a bowl-like pit, a crudely circular orifice with a scant two miles across its rippling rim. There was faint light here to mark the presence of the living intruders. The blue glow radiance of Morrell tube lights under a spread of glassite.

The Grantline camp stood midway up one of the inner cliff walls of the little crater. The broken, rock-strewn floor, two miles wide, lay five hundred feet below the camp. Behind it, the jagged, precipitous cliff rose another five hundred to the heights of the upper rim. A broad level shelf hung midway up the cliff, and upon it Grantline had built his little group of glassite dome shelters. Viewed from above there was the darkly purple crater floor, the upflung circular rim where the Earthlight tinged the spires and crags with yellow sheen; and on the shelf, like a huddled group of birds' nests, Grantline's domes hung and gazed down upon the inner valley.

The air here on the Moon surface was negligible - a scant one five-thousandth of the atmospheric pressure at the sea level on Earth. But within the glassite shelter, a normal Earth pressure must be maintained. Rigidly braced double walls to withstand the explosive tendency, with no external pressure to counteract it. A tremendous necessity for mechanical equipment had burdened Grantline's small ship to capacity. The chemistry of manufactured air, the pressure equalizers, renewers, respirators, the lighting and temperature maintenance of a space-flyer was here.

There was this main Grantline building, stretched low and rectngular along the front edge of the ledge. Within it were living rooms, mess hall and kitchen. Fifty feet behind it, connected by a narrow passage of glassite, was a similar though smaller structure. The mechanical control rooms, with their humming, vibrating mechanisms were here. And an instrument room with signaling apparatus, senders, receivers, mirror-grids and audiphones of several varieties. And an electro-telescope, small but modern, with dome overhead like a little Earth observatory.

From this instrument building, beside the connecting pedestrian passage, wire cables for light, and air tubes and strings and bundles of instrument wires ran to the main structure - gray snakes upon the porous, gray Lunar rock.

The third building seemed a lean-to banked against the cliff wall, a slanting shed-wall of glassite fifty feet high and two hundred in length. Under it, for months Grantline's bores had dug into the cliff. Braced tunnels were here, penetrating back and downward into the vein of rock.

The work was over. The borers had been dismantled and packed away. At one end of the cliff the mining equipment lay piled in a litter. There was a heap of discarded ore where Grantline had carted and dumped it after his first crude refining process had yielded it as waste. The ore slag lay like gray powder flakes strewn down the cliff. Trucks and ore carts along the ledge stood discarded, mute evidence of the weeks and months of work these helmeted miners had undergone, struggling upon this airless, frowning world.

But now all that was finished. The catalytic ore was sufficiently concentrated. It lay - this treasure - in a seventy foot pile behind the glassite lean-to, with a cage of wires over it and an insulation barrage hiding its presence.

The ore shelter was dark; the other two buildings were lighted. And there were small lights mounted at intervals about the camp and along the edge of the ledge. A spider ladder, with tiny platforms some twenty feet one above the other, hung precariously to the cliff-face. It descended the five hundred feet to the crater floor; and, behind the camp, it mounted the jagged cliff-face to the upper rim height, where a small observatory platform was placed.

Such was the outer aspect of the Grantline Treasure Camp near the beginning of this Lunar night, when, unknown to Grantline and his men, the *Planetara* with its brigands was approaching. The night was perhaps a sixth advanced. Full night. No breath of cloud to mar the brilliant starry heavens. The quadrant Earth hung poised like a giant mellow moon over Grantline's crater. A bright Earth, yet no air was here on this Lunar surface to spread its light. Only a glow, mingling with the spots of blue tube light on the poles along the cliff, and the radiance from the lighted buildings.

No evidence of movement showed about the silent camp. Then a pressure door in an end of the main building opened its tiny series of locks. A bent figure came out. The lock closed. The figure straightened and gazed about the camp. Grotesque, bloated semblance of a man! Helmeted, with rounded dome hood, suggestion of an ancient sea diver, yet goggled and trunked like a gas-masked fighter of the twentieth century.

He stopped presently and disconnected metal weights which were upon his shoes.

Then he stood erect again, and with giant strides bounded along the cliff. Fantastic figure in the blue lit gloom! A child's dream of crags and rocks and strange lights with a single monstrous figure in seven league boots.

He went the length of the ledge with his twenty foot strides, inspected the lights, and made adjustments. Came back, and climbed with agile, bounding leaps up the spider ladder to the dome of the crater top. A light flashed on up there. Then it was extinguished.

The goggled, bloated figure came leaping down after a moment. Grantline's exterior watchman making his rounds. He came back to the main building. Fastened the weights on his shoes. Signaled.

The lock opened. The figure went inside.

It was early evening. After the dinner hour and before the time of sleep according to the camp routine Grantline was maintaining. Nine P.M. of Earth Eastern American time, recorded now upon his Earth chronometer. In the living room of the main building Johnny Grantline sat with a dozen of his men dispersed about the room, whiling away as best they could the lonesome hours.

"All as usual. This cursed Moon! When I get home - if I ever do -"

"Say your say, Wilks. But you'll spend your share of the gold leaf and thank your constellations that you had your chance to make it."

"Let him alone! Come on, Wilks, take a hand here. This game is not any good with three."

The man who had been outside flung his hissing helmet recklessly to the floor and unsealed his suit. "Here, get me out of this. No, I won't play. I can't play your cursed game with nothing at stake!"

A laugh went up at the sharp look Johnny Grantline flung from where he sat reading in a corner of the room.

"Commander's orders. No gambling gold leafers tolerated here."

"Play the game, Wilks," Grantline said quietly. "We all know it's infernal - this doing nothing."

"He's been struck by Earthlight," another man laughed. "Commander, I told you not to let that guy Wilks out at night."

A rough but good-natured lot of men. Jolly and raucous by nature in their leisure hours. But there was too much leisure here now. Their mirth had a hollow sound. In older times, explorers of the frozen Polar zones had to cope with inactivity, loneliness and despair. But at least they were on their native world. The grimness of the Moon was eating into the courage of Grantline's men. An unreality here. A weirdness. These fantastic crags. The deadly silence. The nights, almost two weeks of Earth time in length, congealed by the deadly frigidity of space. The days of black sky, blazing stars and flaming Sun, with no atmosphere to diffuse the Sun's heat radiating so swiftly from the naked Lunar surface that the outer temperature still was cold. And day and night, always the beloved Earth disc hanging poised up near the zenith. From thinnest crescent to full Earth, then back to crescent.

All so abnormal, irrational, disturbing to human senses.

With the mining work over, an irritability grew upon Grantline's men. And perhaps since the human mind is so wonderful, elusive a thing, there lay upon these men an indefinable sense of disaster. Johnny Grantline felt it. He thought about it now as he sat in the room corner watching Wilks being forced into the plaget game, and he found the premonition strong within him. Unreasonably, ominous depression! Barring the accident which had disabled his little spaceship when they reached this small crater hole, his expedition had gone well. His instruments, and the information he had from the former explorers, had enabled him to pick up the catalyst vein with only one month of search.

The vein had now been exhausted; but the treasure was here - enough to supply every need on his Earth! Nothing was left but to wait for the *Planetara*. The men were talking of that now.

"She ought to be well midway from Ferrok-Shahn by now. When do you figure she'll be back here and signal us?"

"Twenty days. Give her another five now to Mars, and five in port. That's ten. We'll pick her signals in three weeks, mark me!"

"Three weeks. Just give me three weeks of reasonable sunrise and sunset! This cursed Moon! You mean, Williams, next daylight."

"Ha! He's inventing a Lunar language. You'll be a Moon man yet."

Olaf Swenson, the big blond fellow from the Scandia fiords, came and flung himself down beside Grantline.

"Ay tank they bane without enough to do, Commander -"

"Three weeks isn't very long, Ole."

"No. Maybe not."

From across the room somebody was saying, "If the *Comet* hadn't smashed on us, damn me but I'd ask the Commander to let some of us take her back."

"Shut up, Billy. She *is* smashed."

"You all agreed to things as they are," Johnny said shortly. "We all took the same chances - voluntarily."

A dynamic little fellow, this Johnny Grantline. Short of temper sometimes, but always just, and a perfect leader of men. In stature he was almost as small as Snap. But he was thick-set, with a smooth-shaven, keen-eyed, square-jawed face; and a shock of brown tousled hair. A man of thirty-five, though the decision of his manner, the quiet dominance of his voice made him seem older. He stood up now, surveying the blue lit glassite room with its low ceiling close overhead. He was bow-legged; in movement he seemed to roll with a stiff-legged gait like some sea captains of former days on the deck of his swaying ship. Odd looking figure! Heavy flannel shirt and trousers, boots heavily weighted, and bulky metal-loaded belt strapped about his waist.

He grinned at Swenson. "When the time comes to divide this treasure, everyone will be happy, Ole."

The treasure was estimated to be the equivalent of ninety millions in gold leaf. A hundred and ten millions in the gross as it now stood, with twenty millions to be deducted by the Federated Refiners for reducing it to the standard purity for commercial use. Ninety millions, with only a million and a half to come off for expedition expenses, and the *Planetara's* share another million. A nice little stake.

Grantline strode across the room with his rolling gait.

"Cheer up, boys. Who's winning there? I say, you fellows -"

An audiphone buzzer interrupted him, a call from the duty man in the instrument room of the nearby building.

Grantline clicked the receiver. The room fell into silence. Any call was unusual - nothing ever happened here in the camp.

The duty man's voice sounded over the room.

"Signals coming! Not clear. Will you come over, Commander?"

Signals!

It was never Grantline's way to enforce needless discipline. He offered no objection when every man in the camp rushed through the connecting passages. They crowded the instrument room where the tense duty man sat bending over his radio receivers. The mirrors were swaying.

The duty man looked up and met Grantline's gaze.

"I ran it up to the highest intensity, Commander. We ought to get it -"

"Low scale, Peter?"

"Yes. Weakest infra-red. I'm bringing it up, even though it uses too much of our power."

"Get it," said Grantline shortly.

"I got one slight television swing a minute ago - then it faded. I think it's the *Planetara.*"

"*Planetara*!" The crowding group of men chorused. How could it be the *Planetara*?

But it was. The call came in presently. Unmistakably the *Planetara*, turned back now from her course to Ferrok-Shahn.

"How far away, Peter?"

The duty man consulted the needles of his dial scale. "Close! Very weak infra-red. But close. Around thirty thousand miles, maybe. It's Snap Dean calling."

The *Planetara* here within thirty thousand miles! Excitement and pleasure swept the room. The *Planetara* had for so long been awaited eagerly!

The excitement communicated to Grantline. It was unlike him to be incautious; yet now with no thought save that some unforeseen and pleasing circumstance had brought the *Planetara* ahead of time; incautious, Grantline certainly was!

"Raise the barrage."

"I'll go. My suit is here."

A willing volunteer rushed out to the shed.

"Can you send, Peter?" Grantline demanded.

"Yes. With more power."

"Use it."

Johnny dictated the message of his location which we received. In his incautious excitement he ignored the secret code.

An interval passed. No message had come from us - just Snap's routine signal in the weak infra-red, which we hoped Grantline would not get.

The men crowding Grantline's instrument room waited in tense silence. Then Grantline tried the television again. Its current weakened the lights with the drain upon the distributors, and cooled the room with a sudden deadly chill as the Erentz insulating system slowed down.

The duty man looked frightened. "You'll bulge out our walls, Commander. The internal pressure -"

"We'll chance it."

They picked up the image of the *Planetara*. It shone clear on the grid - the segment of star-field with a tiny cigar-shaped blob. Clear enough to be unmistakable. The *Planetara*! Here now, over the Moon, almost directly overhead, poised at what the altimeter scale showed to be a fraction under thirty thousand miles.

The men gazed in awed silence. The *Planetara* coming....

But the altimeter needle was motionless. The *Planetara* was hanging poised.

A sudden gasp went about the room. The men stood with whitening faces, gazing at the *Planetara's* image. And at the altimeter's needle. It was moving now. The *Planetara* was descending. But not with an orderly swoop.

The grid showed the ship clearly. The bow tilted up, then dipped down. But then in a moment it swung up again. The ship turned partly over. Righted itself. Then swayed again, drunkenly.

The watching men were stricken in horrified silence. The *Planetara's* image momentarily, horribly, grew larger. Swaying. Then turning completely over, rotating slowly end over end.

The *Planetara*, out of control, was falling!

XXI

On the *Planetara*, in the radio room, Snap and I stood with Moa's weapon upon us. Miko held Anita. Triumphant, possessive. Then as she struggled, a gentleness came to this strange Martian giant. Perhaps he really loved her. Looking back on it, I sometimes think so.

"Anita, do not fear me." He held her away from him. "I would not harm you. I want your love." Irony came to him. "And I thought I had killed you. But it was only your brother."

He partly turned. I was aware of how alert was his attention. He grinned. "Hold them, Moa. Don't let them do anything foolish.... So, little Anita, you were masquerading to spy on me? That was wrong of you."

Anita had not spoken. She held herself tensely away from Miko. She had flashed me a look, just one. What horrible mischance to have brought on this catastrophe!

The completion of Grantline's message had come unnoticed by us all. We remained tense.

"Look! Grantline again!" Snap said abruptly.

But the mirrors were steadying. We had no recording mechanism; the rest of the message was lost.

No further message came. There was an interval while Miko

waited. He held Anita in the hollow of his great arm.

"Quiet, little bird. Do not fear me. I have work to do, Anita, this is our great adventure. We will be rich, you and I. All the luxuries these worlds can offer - all for us when this is over. Careful, Moa! This Haljan has no wit."

Well could he say it. I, who had been so witless as to let this come upon us! Moa's weapon prodded me. Her voice hissed at me with all the venom of a reptile enraged. "So that was your game, Gregg Haljan! And I was so graceless as to admit love for you!"

Snap murmured in my ear, "Don't move, Gregg! She's reckless."

She heard it. She whirled on him. "We have lost George Prince, it seems. Well, we will survive without his scientific knowledge. And you, Dean - and this Haljan, mark me - I will kill you both if you cause trouble!"

Miko was gloating. "Don't kill them yet, Moa. What was it Grantline said? Near the crater of Archimedes. Ring us down, Haljan. We'll land."

He signaled the turret, gave Coniston the Grantline message, and audiphoned it below to Hahn. The news spread about the ship. The bandits were jubilant.

"We'll land now, Haljan. Come, Anita and I will go with you to the turret."

I found my voice. "To what destination?"

"Near Archimedes. The Apennine side. Keep well away from the Grantline camp. We will probably sight it as we descend."

There was no trajectory needed. We were almost over Archimedes now. I could drop us with a visible, instrumental course. My mind was whirling with a confusion of thoughts. What could we do? I met Snap's gaze.

"Ring us down, Gregg," he said quietly.

I nodded. I pushed Moa's weapon away. "You don't need that -"

We went to the turret. Moa watched me and Snap, a grim, cold Amazon. She avoided looking at Anita, whom Miko helped down the ladders with a strange mixture of courtierlike grace and amused irony. Coniston stared at Anita.

"I say, not George Prince? The girl -"

"No time for explanations," Miko commanded. "It's the girl, masquerading as her brother. Get below, Coniston. Haljan takes us down."

The astounded Englishman continued to gaze at Anita. But he said, "I mean to say, where to on the Moon? Not to encounter Grantline at once, Miko? Our equipment is not ready."

"Of course not. We will land well away -"

The reluctant Coniston left us. I took the controls. Miko, still holding Anita as though she were a child, sat beside me. "We will watch him, Anita. A skilled fellow at this sort of work."

I rang my signals for the shifting of the gravity plates. The answer should have come from below within a second or two. But it did not. Miko regarded me with his great bushy eyebrows upraised.

"Ring again, Haljan."

I duplicated. No answer. The silence was ominous.

Miko muttered, "That accursed Hahn. Ring again!"

I sent the imperative emergency demand.

No answer. A second or two. Then all of us in the turret were startled. Transfixed. From below came a sudden hiss. It sounded in the turret; it came from the shifting room call grid. The hissing of the pneumatic valves of the plate shifters in the lower control room. The valves were opening; the plates automatically shifting into neutral, and disconnecting!

An instant of startled silence. Miko may have realized the significance of what had happened. Certainly Snap and I did. The hissing ceased. I gripped the emergency plate shifter switch which hung over my head. Its disc was dead! The plates were dead in neutral: in the position they were placed only in port! And their shifting mechanisms were imperative!

I was on my feet. "We're in neutral!"

The Moon disc moved visibly as the *Planetara* lurched. The vault of the heavens was slowly swinging.

Miko ripped out a heavy oath. "Haljan! What is this?"

The heavens turned with a giant swoop. The Moon was over us. It swung in a dizzying arc. Overhead, then back past our stern; under us, then appearing over our bow.

The *Planetara* had turned over. Upending. Rotating, end over end.

For a moment I think all of us in the turret stood and clung. The Moon disc, the Earth, Sun and all the stars were swinging past our windows. So horribly dizzying. The *Planetara* seemed lurching and tumbling. But it was an optical effect only. I stared with grim determination at my feet. The turret seemed to steady.

Then I looked again. That horrible swoop of all the heavens! And the Moon, as it went past seemed expanded. We were falling! Out of control, with the Moon gravity pulling us down!

"That accursed Hahn -"

A moment only had passed. My fancy that the Moon disc was enlarged was merely the horror of my imagination. We had not fallen far enough for that.

But we were falling. Unless I could do something, we would crash upon the Lunar surface.

Anita, killed in this turret: the end of everything - every hope.

Action came to me. I gasped, "Miko, you stay here! The controls are dead! You stay here and hold Anita -"

I ignored Moa's weapon. Snap thrust her away.

"We're falling, you fool - let us alone!"

Miko gasped, "Can you - check us? What happened?"

"I don't know -"

I stood clinging. This dizzying whirl. From the audiphone grid Coniston's voice sounded.

"I say, Haljan, something's wrong. Hahn doesn't signal."

The lookout in the forward tower was clinging to our window. On the deck below our turret a member of the crew appeared, stood lurching for a moment, then shouted and ran, swaying, aimless. From the lower hull corridors our grids sounded with the tramping of running steps. Panic among the crew was spreading over the ship. A chaos below deck.

I pulled at the emergency switch again. Dead....

"Snap, we must get down. The signals."

Coniston's voice came like a scream from the grid. "Hahn is dead. The controls are broken!"

I shouted, "Miko, hold Anita! Come on, Snap!"

We clung to the ladders. Snap was behind me. "Careful, Gregg! Good God!"

This dizzying whirl. I tried not to look. The deck under me was now a blurred kaleidoscope of swinging patches of moonlight and shadow.

We reached the deck. It seemed that from the turret Anita's voice followed us. "Be careful!"

Once inside the ship, our senses steadied. With the rotating, reeling heavens shut out, there were only the shouts and tramping steps of the panic-stricken crew to mark that there was anything amiss. That, and a pseudo sensation of lurching caused by the pulsing of gravity - a pull when the Moon was beneath our hull to combine its forces with our magnetizers; a lightening, when it was overhead. A throbbing, pendulum lurch!

We ran down to the corridor incline. A white-faced member of the crew came running up.

"What's happened, Haljan? What's happened?"

"We're falling!" I gripped him. "Get below. Come with us."

But he jerked away from me. "Falling?"

A steward came running. "Falling? My God!"

Snap swung at them. "Get ahead of us! The manual controls - our only chance - we need all you men at the compressor pumps!"

But it was instinct to try and get on deck, as though here below we were rats caught in a trap. The men tore away from us and ran. Their shouts of panic resounded through the dim, blue lit corridors.

Coniston came lurching from the control room. "I say - falling! Haljan, my God, look!"

Hahn was sprawled at the gravity plate switchboard. Sprawled, head down. Dead. Killed? Or a suicide?

I bent over him. His hands gripped the main switch. He had ripped it loose. And his left hand had reached and broken the fragile line of tubes that intensified the current of the pneumatic plate-shifters. A suicide? With his last frenzy, determined to kill us all? Why?

Then I saw that Hahn had been killed! Not a suicide! In his hand he gripped a small segment of black fabric, a piece torn from an invisible cloak!

Snap was rigging the hand compressors. If he could get the pressure back in the tanks....

I swung on Coniston. "You armed?"

"Yes." He was white-faced and confused, but not in a panic. He showed me his heat ray cylinder. "What do you want me to do?"

"Round up the crew. Get all you can. Bring them here to man the pumps."

He dashed away. Snap called after him, "Kill them if they argue!"

Miko's voice sounded from the turret call grid: "Falling!

Haljan, you can see it now! Check us!"

Desperate moments. Or was it an hour? Coniston brought the men. He stood over them with menacing weapon.

We had all the pumps going. The pressure rose a little in the tanks. Enough to shift a bow plate. I tried it. The plate slowly clicked into a new combination. A gravity repulsion just in the bow-tip.

I signaled Miko. "Have we stopped swinging?"

"No. But slower."

I could feel it, that lurch of the gravity. But not steady now. A limp. The tendency of our bow was to stay up.

"More pressure, Snap."

One of the crew rebelled, tried to bolt from the room.

Coniston shot him down.

I shifted another bow plate. Then two in the stern. The stern plates seemed to move more readily than the others.

"Run all the stern plates," Snap advised.

I tried it. The lurching stopped. Miko called, "We're bow down. Falling!"

But not falling free. The Moon gravity pull on us was more than half neutralized.

"I'll go up, Snap, and try the engines. You don't mind staying down here? Executing my signals?"

"You idiot!" He gripped my shoulders. His eyes were gleaming, his face haggard, but his pale lips twitched with a smile.

"Maybe it's good-bye, Gregg. We'll fall - fighting."

"Yes. Fighting. Coniston, you keep the pressure up."

With the broken tubes it took nearly all the pressure to maintain the few plates I had shifted. One slipped back to neutral. Then the pumps gained on it, and it shifted again.

I dashed up to the deck. Oh, the Moon was so close now! So horribly close! The deck shadows were still. Through the forward bow windows the Moon surface glared up at us.

Those last horrible minutes were a blur. And there was always Anita's face. She left Miko. Faced with death, he sat clinging. Moa too, sat apart - staring.

And Anita crept to me. "Gregg, dear one. The end...."

I tried the electronic engines from the stern, setting them in reverse. The streams of their light glowed from the stern, forward along our hull, and flared down from our bow toward the Lunar surface. But no atmosphere was here to give resistance. Perhaps the electronic streams checked our fall a little. The pumps gave us pressure just in the last minutes, to slide a few of the hull plates. But our bow stayed down. We slid, like a spent rocket falling.

I recall the horror of that expanding Lunar surface. The maw of Archimedes yawning. A blob. Widening to a great pit. Then I saw it was to one side, rushing upward.

"Gregg, dear one - good-bye."

Her gentle arms about me. The end of everything for us. I recall murmuring, "Not falling free, Anita. Some hull plates are set."

My dials showed another plate shifting, checking us a little further. Good old Snap!

I calculated the next best plate to shift. I tried it. Slid it over.

Then everything faded but the feeling of Anita's arms around me.

"Gregg, dear one -"

The end of everything for us....

There was an up-rush of gray-black rock.

XXII

I opened my eyes to a dark blur of confusion. My shoulder hurt - a pain shooting through it. Something lay like a weight on me. I could not seem to move my left arm. Then I moved it and it hurt. I was lying twisted. I sat up. And with a rush, memory came. The crash was over. I was not dead. Anita -

She was lying beside me. There was a little light here in the silent blur - a soft mellow Earthlight filtering in the window. The weight on me was Anita. She lay sprawled, her head and shoulders half way across my lap.

Not dead! Thank God, not dead! She moved. Her arms went around me, and I lifted her. The Earthlight glowed on her pale face.

"It's past, Anita! We've struck, and we're still alive."

I held her as though all of life's turgid dangers were powerless to touch us.

But in the silence my floating senses were brought back to reality by a faint sound forcing itself upon me. A little hiss. The faintest murmuring breath like a hiss. Escaping air!

I cast off Anita's clinging arms. "Anita, this is madness!"

For minutes we must have been lying there in the heaven of our embrace. But air was escaping! The *Planetara's* dome was broken and our precious air was hissing out.

Full reality came to me. I was not seriously injured. I found I could move freely. I could stand. A twisted shoulder, a limp left arm, but they were better in a moment.

And Anita did not seem to be hurt. Blood was upon her. But not her own.

Beside Anita, stretched face down on the turret grid, was the giant figure of Miko. The blood lay in a small pool against his face. A widening pool.

Moa was here. I thought her body twitched; then was still. This soundless wreckage! In the dim glow of the wrecked turret with its two motionless, broken human figures, it seemed as though Anita and I were ghouls prowling. I saw that the turret had fallen over to the *Planetara's* deck. It lay dashed against the dome side.

The deck was aslant. A litter of wreckage! A broken human figure showed - one of the crew who, at the last, must have come running up. The forward observation tower was down on the chart room roof: in its metal tangle I thought I could see the legs of the tower lookout.

So this was the end of the brigands' adventure. The *Planetara's* last voyage! How small and futile are humans' struggles. Miko's daring enterprise - so villainous - brought all in a few moments to this silent tragedy. The *Planetara* had fallen thirty thousand miles. But why? What had happened to Hahn? And where was Coniston, down in this broken hull?

And Snap! I thought suddenly of Snap.

I clutched at my wandering wits. This inactivity was death. The escaping air hissed in my ears. Our precious air, escaping away into the vacant desolation of the Lunar emptiness. Through one of the twisted, slanting dome windows a rocky spire was visible. The *Planetara* lay bow down, wedged in a jagged cradle of Lunar rock. A miracle that the hull and dome had held together.

"Anita, we must get out of here!"

"Their helmets are in the forward storage room, Gregg."

She was staring at the fallen Miko and Moa. She shuddered and turned away and gripped me. "In the forward storage room, by the port of the emergency exit."

If only the exit locks would operate! We must find Snap and get out of here. Good old Snap! Would we find him lying dead?

We climbed from the slanting, fallen turret, over the wreckage of the littered deck. It was not difficult. A lightness was upon us. The *Planetara's* gravity-magnetizers were dead; this was only the light Moon gravity pulling us.

"Careful, Anita. Don't jump too freely."

We leaped along the deck. The hiss of the escaping pressure was like a clanging gong of warning to tell us to hurry. The hiss of death so close!

"Snap -" I murmured.

"Oh, Gregg, I pray we may find him alive!"

With a fifteen foot leap we cleared a pile of broken deck chairs. A man lay groaning near them. I went back with a rush. Not Snap! A steward. He had been a brigand, but he was a steward to me now.

"Get up! This is Haljan. Hurry, we must get out of here The air is escaping!"

But he sank back and lay still. No time to find if I could help him: there was Anita and Snap to save.

We found a broken entrance to one of the descending passages. I flung the debris aside and cleared it. Like a giant of strength with only this Moon gravity holding me, I raised a broken segment of superstructure and heaved it back.

Anita and I dropped ourselves down the sloping passage. The interior of the wrecked ship was silent and dim. An occasional passage light was still burning. The passage and all the rooms lay askew. Wreckage everywhere but the double dome and hull shell had withstood the shock. Then I realized that the Erentz system was slowing down. Our heat, like our air, was escaping, radiating away, a deadly chill settling on everything. The silence and the deadly chill of death would soon be here in these wrecked corridors. The end of the *Planetara*.

We prowled like ghouls. We did not see Coniston. Snap had been by the shifter pumps. We found him in the oval doorway. He lay sprawled. Dead? No, he moved. He sat up before we could get to him. He seemed confused, but his senses clarified with the movement of our figures over him.

"Gregg! Why, Anita!"

"Snap! You're all right? We struck - the air is escaping."

He pushed me away. He tried to stand. "I'm all right. I was up a minute ago. Gregg, it's getting cold. Where is she? I had her here - she wasn't killed. I spoke to her."

Irrational!

"Snap!" I held him. Shook him. "Snap, old fellow!"

He said normally, "Easy, Gregg. I'm all right."

Anita gripped him. "Who, Snap?"

"She - there she is...."

Another figure was here! On the grid floor by the door oval. A figure partly shrouded in a broken invisible cloak and hook. An invisible cloak! I saw a white face with opened eyes regarding me.

"Venza!" I bent down. "You!"

Venza here? Why ... how ... my thoughts swept on. Venza here - dying? Her eyes closed. But she murmured to Anita, "Where is he? I want him."

I murmured impulsively, "Here I am, Venza dear." Gently, as one would speak with gentle sympathy to humor the dying. "Here I am, Venza."

But it was only the confusion of the shock upon her. And it was upon us all. She pushed at Anita. "I want him." She saw me; this whimsical Venus girl! Even here as we gathered, all of us blurred by shock, confused in the dim, wrecked ship with the chill of death coming - even here she could jest. Her pale lips smiled.

"You, Gregg. I'm not hurt - I don't think I'm hurt." She managed to get herself up on one elbow. "Did you think I wanted you with my dying breath? What conceit! Not you, Handsome Haljan! I was calling Snap."

He was down to her. "We're all right, Venza. It's over. We must get out of the ship. The air is escaping."

We gathered in the oval doorway. We fought the confusion of panic.

"The exit port is this way."

Or was it? I answered Snap, "Yes, I think so."

The ship suddenly seemed a stranger to me. So cold. So vibrationless. Broken lights. These slanting wrecked corridors. With the ventilating fans stilled, the air was turning fetid. Chilling. And thinning, with escaping pressure, rarefying so that I could feel the grasp of it in my lungs and the pin-pricks in my cheeks.

We started off. Four of us, still alive in this silent ship of death. My blurred thoughts tried to cope with it all. Venza here. I remembered how she had bade me create a diversion when the women passengers were landing on the asteroid. She had carried out her purpose! In the confusion she had not gone ashore. A stowaway here. She had secured the cloak. Prowling, to try and help us, she had come upon Hahn. Had seized his ray cylinder and struck him down, and been herself knocked unconscious by his dying lunge, which also had broken the tubes and wrecked the *Planetara*. And Venza, unconscious, had been lying here with the mechanism of her cloak still operating, so that we did not see her when we came and found why Hahn did not answer my signals.

"It's here, Gregg."

Snap and I lifted the pile of Moon equipment to which she referred. We located four suits and helmets and the mechanisms to operate them.

"More are in the chart room," Anita said.

But we needed no others. I robed Anita and showed her the mechanisms. Snap was helping Venza. We were all stiff from the cold; but within the suits and their pulsing currents, the blessed warmth came again.

The helmets had ports through which food and drink could be taken. I stood with my helmet ready. Anita, Venza and Snap were bloated and grotesque beside me. We had found food and water here, assembled in portable cases which the brigands had prepared. Snap lifted them, and signaled to me he was ready.

My helmet shut out all sounds save my own breathing, my pounding heart, and the murmur of the mechanism. The warmth and pure air were good.

We reached the hull port locks. They operated! We went through in the light of the headlamps over our foreheads.

I closed the locks after us: an instinct to keep the air in the ship for the other trapped humans lying in there.

We slid down the sloping side of the *Planetara*. We were unweighted, irrationally agile with this slight gravity. I fell a dozen feet and landed with barely a jar.

We were out on the Lunar surface. A great sloping ramp of crags stretched down before us. Gray-black rock tinged with Earthlight. The Earth hung amid the stars in the blackness overhead like a huge section of a glowing yellow ball.

This grim, desolate, silent landscape! Beyond the ramp, fifty feet below us, a tumbled naked plain stretched away into blurred distance. But I could see mountains off there. Behind us, the towering, frowning rampart-wall of Archimedes loomed against the sky.

I had turned to look back at the *Planetara*. She lay broken, wedged between spires of upstanding rock. A few of her lights still gleamed. The end of the *Planetara*!

The three grotesque figures of Anita, Venza and Snap had started off. Hunchback figures with the tanks mounted on their shoulders. I bounded and caught them. I touched Snap. We made audiphone contact.

"Which way do you think?" I demanded.

"I think this way, down the ramp. Away from Archimedes, toward the mountains. It shouldn't be too far."

"You run with Venza. I'll hold Anita."

He nodded. "But we must keep together, Gregg."

We could soon run freely. Down the ramp, out over the tumbled plain. Bounding, grotesque, leaping strides. The girls were more agile, more skillful. They were soon leading us. The Earth shadows of their figures leaped beside them. The *Planetara* faded into the distance behind us. Archimedes stood back there. Ahead, the mountains came closer.

An hour perhaps. I lost track of time. Occasionally we stopped to rest. Were we going toward the Grantline camp? Would they see our tiny waving headlights?

Another interval. Then far ahead of us on the ragged plain, lights showed! Moving, tiny spots of light! Headlights on helmeted figures!

We ran, monstrously leaping. A group of figures were off there. Grantline's party? Snap gripped me.

"Grantline! We're safe, Gregg! Safe!"

He took his bulb light from his helmet; we stood in a group while he waved it. A semaphore signal.

"*Grantline?*"

And the answer came, "*Yes. You, Dean?* "

Their personal code. No doubt of this - it was Grantline, who had seen the *Planetara* fall and had come to help us.

I stood then with my hand holding Anita. And I whispered, "It's Grantline! We're safe, Anita, my darling!"

Death had been so close! Those horrible last minutes on the *Planetara* had shocked us, marked us. We stood trembling.

And Grantline and his men came bounding up, weird, inflated figures.

A helmeted figure touched me. I saw through the helmetpane the visage of a stern-faced, square-jawed young man.

"Grantline? Johnny Grantline?"

"Yes," said his voice at my ear-grid. "I'm Grantline. You're Haljan? Gregg Haljan?"

They crowded around us. Gripped us, to hear our explanations.

Brigands! It was amazing to Johnny Grantline. But the menace was over now, over as soon as Grantline realized its existence.

We stood for a brief time discussing it. Then I drew apart, leaving Snap with Grantline. And Anita joined me. I held her arm so that we had audiphone contact.

"Anita, mine."

"Gregg - dear one!"

Murmured nothings which mean so much to lovers!

As we stood in the fantastic gloom of Lunar desolation, with the blessed Earthlight on us, I sent up a prayer of thankfulness. Not that the enormous treasure was saved. Not that the attack upon Grantline had been averted. But only that Anita was given back to me. In moments of greatest emotion the human mind individualizes. To me, there was only Anita.

Life is very strange! The gate to the shining garden of our love seemed swinging wide to let us in. Yet I recall that a vague fear still lay on me. A premonition?

I felt a touch on my arm. A bloated helmet visor was thrust

near my own. I saw Snap's face peering at me.

"Grantline thinks we should return to the *Planetara.* Might find some of them alive."

Grantline touched me. "It's only human -"

"Yes," I said.

We went back. Some ten of us - a line of grotesque figures bounding with slow, easy strides over the jagged, rock-strewn plain. Our lights danced before us.

The *Planetara* came at last into view. My ship. Again that pang swept me as I saw her. This, her last resting place. She lay here, in her open tomb, shattered, broken, unbreathing. The lights on her were extinguished. The Erentz system had ceased to pulse - the heart of the dying ship, for a while beating faintly, but now at rest.

We left the two girls with some of Grantline's men at the admission port. Snap, Grantline and I, with three others, went inside. There still seemed to be air, but not enough so that we dared remove our helmets.

It was dark inside the wrecked ship. The corridors were black. The hull control rooms were dimly with Earthlight straggling through the windows.

This littered tomb. Cold and silent with death. We stumbled over a fallen figure. A member of the crew. Grantline straightened from examining it.

"Dead," he said.

Earthlight fell on the horrible face. Puffed flesh, bloated red from the blood which had oozed from its pores in the thinning air. I looked away.

We prowled further. Hahn lay dead in the pump room. The body of Coniston should have been near here. We did not see it. We climbed up to the slanting, littered deck. The air up here had all almost hissed away.

Again Grantline touched me. "That the turret?"

No wonder he asked me! The wreckage was all so formless.

"Yes."

We climbed after Snap into the broken turret room. We passed the body of that steward who just at the end had appealed to me and I had left dying. The legs of the forward lookout still poked grotesquely up from the wreckage of the observatory tower where it lay smashed down against the roof of the chart room.

We shoved ourselves into the turret. What was this? No bodies here! The giant Miko was gone! The pool of blood lay congealed into a frozen dark splotch on the metal grid.

And Moa was gone! They had not been dead. Had dragged themselves out of here, fighting desperately for life. We would find them somewhere around here.

But we did not. Nor Coniston. I recalled what Anita had said: other suits and helmets had been here in the nearby chart room. The brigands had taken them, and food and water doubtless, and escaped from the ship, following us through the lower admission ports only a few minutes after we were gone.

We made careful search of the entire ship. Eight of the bodies which should have been here were missing: Miko, Moa, Coniston and five of the crew.

We did not find them outside. They were hiding near here, no doubt, more willing to take their chances than to yield to us now. But how, in all this Lunar desolation, could we hope to locate them?

"No use," said Grantline. "Let them go. If they want death, well, they deserve it."

But we were saved. Then, as I stood there, realization leaped at me. Saved? Were we not indeed fatuous fools?

In all these emotion-swept moments since we had encountered Grantline, memory of that brigand ship coming from Mars had never once occurred to Snap and me!

I told Grantline now. He stared at me.

"What!"

I told him again. It would be here in eight days. Fully manned and armed.

"But Haljan, we have almost no weapons! All my *Comet's* space was taken with equipment and the mechanisms for my camp. I can't signal Earth! I was depending on the *Planetara*!"

It surged upon us. The brigand menace past? We were blindly congratulating ourselves on our safety! But it would be eight days or more before in distant Ferrok-Shahn the nonarrival of the *Planetara* would cause any real comment. No one was searching for us - no one was worried over us.

No wonder the crafty Miko was willing to take his chances out here in the Lunar wilds! His ship, his reinforcements, his weapons were coming rapidly!

And we were helpless. Almost unarmed. Marooned here on the Moon!

XXIII

"Try it again," Snap urged. "Good God, Johnny, we've got to raise some Earth station! Chance it! Use the power - run it up full. Chance it!"

We were gathered in Grantline's instrument room. The duty man, with blanched grim face, sat at his senders. The Grantline crew shoved close around us. There were very few observers in the high-powered Earth stations who knew that an exploring party was on the Moon. Perhaps none of them. The Government officials who had sanctioned the expedition and Halsey and his confreres in the Detective Bureau were not anticipating trouble at this point. The *Planetara* was supposed to be well on her course to Ferrok-Shahn. It was when she was due to return that Halsey would be alert.

Grantline used his power far beyond the limits of safety. He cut down the lights; the telescope intensifiers and television were completely disconnected; the ventilators were momentarily stilled, so that the air here in the little room crowded with men rapidly grew fetid. All, to save power pressure, that the vital Erentz system might survive.

Even so, it was strained to the danger point. Our heat was radiating away; the deadly chill of space crept in.

"Again!" ordered Grantline.

The duty man flung on the power in rhythmic pulses. In the

silence, the tubes hissed. The light sprang through the banks of rotating prisms, intensified up the scale until, with a vague, almost invisible beam, it left the last swaying mirror and leaped through our overhead dome and into space.

"Enough," said Grantline. "Switch it off. We'll let it go at that for now."

It seemed that every man in the room had been holding his breath in the chill darkness. The lights came on again; the Erentz motors accelerated to normal. The strain on the walls eased up, and the room began warming.

Had the Earth caught our signal? We did not want to waste the power to find out. Our receivers were disconnected. If an answering signal came, we could not know it. One of the men said:

"Let's assume they read us." He laughed, but it was a high-pitched, tense laugh. "We don't dare even use the telescope or television. Or electron radio. Our rescue ship might be right overhead, visible to the naked eye, before we see it. Three days more - that's what I'll give it."

But the three days passed and no rescue ship came. The Earth was almost at the full. We tried signaling again. Perhaps it got through - we did not know. But our power was weaker now. The wall of one of the rooms sprang a leak, and the men were hours repairing it. I did not say so, but never once did I feel that our signals were read on Earth. Those cursed clouds! The Earth almost everywhere seemed to have poor visibility.

Four of our eight days of grace were all too soon passed. The brigand ship must be half way here by now.

They were busy days for us. If we could have captured Miko and his band, our danger would have been less imminent. With the treasure insulated, and our camp in darkness, the arriving brigand ship might never find us. But Miko knew our location; he would signal his oncoming ship when it was close and lead it to us.

During those three days - and the days which followed them – Grantline sent out searching parties. But it was unavailing. Miko, Moa and Coniston, with their five underlings, could not be found.

We had at first hoped that the brigands might have perished. But that was soon dispelled! I went - about the third day - with the party that was sent to the *Planetara*. We wanted to salvage some of its equipment, its unbroken power units. And Snap and I had worked out an idea which we thought might be of service. We needed some of the *Planetara's* smaller gravity plate sections. Those in Grantline's wrecked little *Comet* had stood so long that their radiations had gone dead. But the *Planetara's* were still working.

Our hope that Miko might have perished was dashed. He too had returned to the *Planetara*! The evidence was clear before us. The vessel was stripped of all its power units save those which were dead and useless. The last of the food and water stores were taken. The weapons in the chart room - the Benson curve lights, projectors and heat rays - had vanished!

Other days passed. Earth reached the full and was waning. The fourteen day Lunar night was in its last half. No rescue ship came from Earth. We had ceased our efforts to signal, for we needed all our power to maintain ourselves. The camp would be in a state of siege before long. That was the best we could hope for. We had a few short-range weapons, such as Bensons, heat-rays and projectors. A few hundred feet of effective range was the most any of them could obtain. The heat-rays - in giant form one of the most deadly weapons on Earth - were only slowly efficacious on the airless Moon. Striking an intensely cold surface, their warming radiations were slow to act. Even in a blasting heat beam a man in his Erentz helmet-suit could withstand the ray for several minutes.

We were, however, well equipped with explosives. Grantline had brought a large supply for his mining operations, and much of it was still unused. We had, also, an ample stock of oxygen fuses, and a variety of oxygen light flares in small, fragile glass globes.

It was to use these explosives against the brigands that Snap and I were working out our scheme with the gravity plates. The brigand ship would come with giant projectors and some thirty men. If we could hold out against them for a time, the fact that the *Planetara* was missing would bring us help from Earth.

Another day. A tenseness was upon all of us, despite the absorption of our feverish activities. To conserve power, the camp was almost dark, we lived in dim, chill rooms, with just a few weak spots of light outside to mark the watchmen on their rounds. We did not use the telescope, but there was scarcely an hour when one or the other of the men was not sitting on a cross-piece up in the dome of the little instrument room, casting a tense, searching gaze through his glasses into the black, starry firmament. A ship might appear at any time now - a rescue ship from Earth, or the brigands from Mars.

Anita and Venza through these days could aid us very little save by their cheering words. They moved about the rooms, trying to inspire us; so that all the men, when they might have been humanly sullen and cursing their fate, were turned to grim activity, or grim laughter, making a joke of the coming siege. The morale of the camp now was perfect. An improvement indeed over the inactivity of their former peaceful weeks!

Grantline mentioned it to me. "Well put up a good fight, Haljan. These fellows from Mars will know they've had a task before they ever sail off with the treasure."

I had many moments alone with Anita. I need not mention them. It seemed that our love was crossed by the stars, with an adverse fate dooming it. And Snap and Venza must have felt the same. Among the men, we were always quietly, grimly active. But alone.... I came upon Snap once with his arms around the little Venus girl. I heard him say:

"Accursed luck! That you and I should find each other too late, Venza. We could have a lot of fun in Greater New York together."

"Snap, we will!"

As I turned away, I murmured, "And pray God, so will Anita and I."

The girls slept together in a small room of the main building. Often during the time of sleep, when the camp was stilled except for the night watch, Snap and I would sit in the corridor near the girls' door, talking of that time when we would all be back on our blessed Earth.

Our eight days of grace were passed. The brigand ship was due - now, tomorrow, or the next day.

I recall, that night, my sleep was fitfully uneasy. Snap and I had a cubby together. We talked, and made futile plans. I went to sleep, but awakened after a few hours. Impending disaster lay heavily upon me. But there was nothing abnormal nor unusual in that!

Snap was asleep. I was restless, but I did not have the heart to awaken him. He needed what little repose he could get. I dressed, left our cubby and wandered out into the corridor of the main building.

It was cold in the corridor, and gloomy with the weak blue light. An interior watchman passed me.

"All as usual, Haljan."

"Nothing in sight?"

"No. They're watching."

I went through the connecting corridor to the adjacent building. In the instrument room several of the men were gathered, scanning the vault overhead.

"Nothing, Haljan."

I stayed with them awhile, then wandered away. An outside man met me near the admission lock chambers of the main building. The duty man here sat at his controls, raising the air pressure in the locks through which the outside watchman was coming. The relief sat here in his bloated suit, with his helmet on his knees. It was Wilks.

"Nothing yet, Haljan. I'm going up to the peak of the crater to see if anything is in sight. I wish that damnable brigand ship would come and get it over with."

Instinctively we all spoke in half whispers, the tenseness bearing in on us.

The outside man was white and grim, but he grinned at Wilks. He tried the familiar jest: "Don't let the Earthlight get you!"

Wilks went out through the ports - a process of no more than a minute. I wandered away again through the corridors.

I suppose it was half an hour later that I chanced to be gazing through a corridor window. The lights along the rocky cliff were tiny blue spots. The head of the stairway leading down to the abyss of the crater floor was visible. The bloated figure of Wilks was just coming up. I watched him for a moment making his rounds. He did not stop to inspect the lights. That was routine. I thought it odd that he passed them.

Another minute passed. The figure of Wilks went with slow bounds over toward the back of the ledge where the glassite shelter housed the treasure. It was all dark off there. Wilks went into the gloom, but before I lost sight of him, he came back. As though he had changed his mind, he headed for the foot of the staircase which led up the cliff to where, at the peak of the little crater, five hundred feet above us, the narrow observatory was perched. He climbed with easy bounds, the light on his helmet bobbing in the gloom.

I stood watching. I could not tell why there seemed to be something queer about Wilks' actions. But I was struck with it, nevertheless. I watched him disappear over the summit.

Another minute went by. Wilks did not reappear. I thought I could make out his light on the platform up there. Then abruptly a tiny white beam was waving from the observatory platform! It flashed once or twice, then was extinguished. And now I saw Wilks plainly, standing in the Earthlight, gazing down.

Queer actions! Had the Earthlight touched him? Or was that a local signal call which he sent out? Why should Wilks be signaling? What was he doing with a hand helio? Our watchmen, I knew, had no reason to carry one.

And to whom could Wilks be signaling? To whom, across this Lunar desolation? The answer stabbed at me: to Miko's band!

I waited less than a moment. No further light. Wilks was still up there!

I went back to the lock entrance. Spare helmets and suits were here beside the keeper. He gazed at me inquiringly.

"I'm going out, Franck. Just for a minute." It struck me that perhaps I was a meddlesome fool. Wilks, of all of Grantline's men, was, I knew, most in his commander's trust. The signal could have been some part of this night's ordinary routine, for all I knew.

I was hastily donning an Erentz suit. I added, "Let me out. I just got the idea Wilks is acting strangely." I laughed. "Maybe the Earthlight has touched him."

With my helmet on, I went through the locks. Once outside, with the outer panel closed behind me, I dropped the weights from my belt and shoes and extinguished my helmet light.

Wilks was still up there. Apparently he had not moved. I bounded off across the ledge to the foot of the ascending stairs. Did Wilks see me coming? I could not tell. As I approached the stairs the platform was cut off from my line of vision.

I mounted with bounding leaps. In my flexible gloved hand I carried my only weapon, a small projector with firing caps for use in this outside near-vacuum.

I held the weapon behind me. I would talk to Wilks first. I went slowly up the last hundred feet. Was Wilks still up there? The summit was bathed in Earthlight. The little metal observatory platform came into view above my head.

Wilks was not there. Then I saw him standing on the rocks nearby, motionless. But in a moment he saw me coming.

I waved my left hand with a gesture of greeting. It seemed to me that he started, made as though to leap away, and then changed his mind. I sailed from the head of the staircase with a twenty foot leap and landed lightly beside him. I gripped his arm for audiphone contact.

"Wilks!"

Through my visor his face was visible. I saw him and he saw me. And I heard his voice:

"You, Haljan. How nice!"

It was not Wilks, but the brigand Coniston.

XXIV

The duty man at the exit locks stood at his window and watched me curiously. He saw me go up the spider stairs. He could see the figure he thought was Wilks, standing at the top. He saw me join Wilks, saw us locked together in combat.

For a brief instant the duty man stood amazed. There were two fantastic figures, fighting at the very brink of the cliff. They were small, dwarfed by distance, alternately dim and bright as they swayed in and out of the shadows. The duty man could not tell one from the other. To him it was Haljan and Wilks, fighting to the death!

The duty man sprang into action. An interior siren call was on the instrument panel near him. He rang it frantically.

The men came rushing to him, Grantline among them.

"What's this? Good God, Franck!"

They had seen the silent, deadly combat up there on the cliff.

Grantline stood stricken with amazement. "That's Wilks!"

"And Haljan," the duty man gasped. "He went out - something wrong with Wilks' actions -"

The interior of the camp was in a turmoil. The men, awakened from sleep, ran out into the corridors shouting questions.

"An attack?"

"Is it an attack?"

"The brigands?"

But it was Wilks and Haljan in a fight up there on the cliff. The men crowded at the bull's-eye windows.

And over all the confusion the alarm siren, with no one thinking to shut it off, was screaming.

Grantline, momentarily stricken, stood gazing. One of the figures broke away from the other, bounded up to the summit from the stair platform to which they had both fallen. The other followed. They locked together, swaying at the brink. For an instant it seemed that they would go over; then they surged back, momentarily out of sight.

Grantline found his wits. "Stop them! I'll go out and stop them! What fools!"

He was hastily donning one of the Erentz suits. "Cut off that siren!"

Within a minute Grantline was ready. The duty man called from the window, "Still at it, the fools. By the infernal - they'll kill themselves!"

"Franck, let me out."

"I'll go with you, Commander." But the volunteer was not equipped. Grantline would not wait.

The duty man turned to his panel. The volunteer shoved a weapon at Grantline.

Grantline jammed on his helmet, took the weapon.

He moved the few steps into the air chamber which was the first of the three pressure locks. Its interior door panel swung open for him. But the door did not close after him!

Cursing the man's slowness, he waited a few seconds. Then he turned to the corridor. The duty man came running.

Grantline took off his helmet. "What in hell -"

"Broken! Dead!"

"What!"

"Smashed from outside," gasped the duty man. "Look there - my tubes -"

The control tubes of the ports had flashed into a short circuit and burned out. The admission ports would not open!

"And the pressure controls smashed! Broken from outside!"

There was no way now of getting through the pressure locks. The doors, the entire pressure lock system, was dead. Had it been tampered with from outside?

As if to answer Grantline's question there came a chorus of shouts from the men at the corridor windows.

"Commander! By God - look!"

A figure was outside, close to the building! Clothed in suit and helmet, it stood, bloated and gigantic. It had evidently been lurking at the port entrance, had ripped out the wires there.

It moved past the windows, saw the staring faces of the men, and made off with giant bounds. Grantline reached the window in time to see it vanish around the building corner.

It was a giant figure, larger than an Earth man. A Martian?

* * * * *

Up on the summit of the crater the two small figures were still fighting. All this turmoil had taken no more than a minute or two.

A lurking Martian outside? The brigand, Miko? More than ever, Grantline was determined to get out. He shouted to his men to don some of the other suits, and called for some of the hand projectors.

But he could not get out through these main admission ports. He could have forced the panels open perhaps; but with the pressure changing mechanism broken, it would merely let the air out of the corridor. A rush of air, probably uncontrollable. How serious the damage was, no one could tell as yet. It would perhaps take hours to repair it.

Grantline was shouting, "Get those weapons! That's a Martian outside! The brigand leader, probably! Get into your suits, anyone who wants to go with me! We'll go by the manual emergency exit."

But the prowling Martian had found it! Within a minute Grantline was there. It was a smaller two-lock gateway of manual control, so that the person going out could operate it himself. It was in a corridor at the other end of the main building. But Grantline was too late! The lever would not open the panels!

Had someone gone out this way and broken the mechanisms after him? A traitor in the camp? Or had someone come in from outside? Or had the skulking Martian outside broken this lock as he had broken the other?

The questions surged on Grantline. His men crowded around him. The news spread. The camp was a prison! No one could get out!

And outside, the skulking Martian had disappeared. But Wilks and Haljan were still fighting. Grantline could see the two figures up on the observatory platform. They bounded apart, then together again. Crazily swaying, bouncing, striking the rail.

They went together in a great leap off the platform onto the rocks, and rolled in a bright patch of Earthlight. First one on top, then the other.

They rolled unheeding to the brink. Here, beyond the midway ledge which held the camp, it was a sheer drop of a thousand feet, on down to the crater floor.

The figures were rolling; then one shook himself loose; rose up, seized the other and, with desperate strength, shoved him -

The victorious figure drew back to safety. The other fell, hurtling down into the shadows past the camp level - down out of sight in the darkness of the crater floor.

Snap, who was in the group near Grantline at the window gasped, "God! Was that Gregg who fell?"

No one could say. No one answered. Outside, on the camp ledge, another helmeted figure now became visible. It was not far from the main building when Grantline first noticed it. It was running fast, bounding toward the spider staircase. It began mounting.

And now still another figure became visible - the giant Martian again. He appeared from around the corner of the main Grantline building. He evidently saw the winner of the combat on the cliff, who now was standing in the Earthlight, gazing down. And he saw too, no doubt, the second figure mounting the stairs. He stood quite near the window through which Grantline and his men were gazing, with his back to the building, looking up to the summit. Then he ran with tremendous leaps toward the ascending staircase.

Was it Haljan standing up there on the summit? Who was it climbing the stairs? And was the third figure Miko?

Grantline's mind framed the questions. But his attention was torn from them, and torn even from the swift silent drama outside. The corridor was ringing with shouts.

"We're imprisoned! Can't get out! Was Haljan killed? The brigands are outside!"

And then an interior audiphone blared a calling for Grantline. Someone in the instrument room of the adjoining building was talking.

"Commander, I tried the telescope to see who got killed -"

But he did not say who got killed, for he had greater news.

"Commander! The brigand ship!"

Miko's reinforcements had come.

XXV

Not Wilks, but Coniston! His drawling, British voice:

"You, Gregg Haljan! How nice!"

His voice broke off as he jerked his arm from me. My hand with the projector came up, but with a sweeping blow he struck my wrist. The weapon dropped to the rocks.

I fought instinctively, those first moments; my mind was whirling with the shock of surprise. This was not Wilks, but the brigand Coniston.

It was an eerie combat. We swayed; shoving, kicking, wrestling. His hold around my middle shut off the Erentz circulation; the warning buzz rang in my ears, to mingle with the rasp of his curses. I flung him off, and my Erentz motors recovered. He staggered away, but in a great leap came at me again.

I was taller, heavier and far stronger than Coniston. But I found him crafty, and where I was awkward in handling my lightness, he seemed more skillfully agile.

I became aware that we were on the twenty foot square grid of the observatory platform. It had a low metal railing. We surged against it. I caught a dizzying glimpse of the abyss. Then it receded as we bounced the other way. And then we fell to the grid. His helmet bashed against mine, striking as though butting with the side of his head to puncture my visor panel. His gloved fingers were clutching at my throat.

As we regained our feet, I flung him off, and bounded like a diver, head first, into him. He went backward, but skillfully kept his feet under him, gripped me again and shoved me.

I was tottering at the head of the staircase - falling. But I clutched at him. We fell some twenty or thirty feet to be next lower spider landing. The impact must have dazed us both. I recall my vague idea that we must have fallen down the cliff.... My air shut off - then it came again. The roaring in my ears was stilled; my head cleared, and I found that we were on the landing, fighting.

He presently broke away from me, bounded to the summit with me after him. In the close confines of the suit I was bathed in sweat and gasping. I had no thought to increase the oxygen control. I could not find it; or it would not operate.

I realized that I was fighting sluggishly, almost aimlessly. But so was Coniston!

It seemed dreamlike. A phantasmagoria of blows and staggering steps. A nightmare with only the horrible vision of this goggled helmet always before my eyes.

It seemed that we were rolling on the ground, back on the summit. The unshadowed Earthlight was clear and bright. The abyss was beside me. Coniston, rolling, was now on top, now under me, trying to shove me over the brink. It was all like a dream - as though I were asleep, dreaming that I did not have enough air.

I strove to keep my senses. He was struggling to roll me over the brink. God, that would not do! But I was so tired. One cannot fight without oxygen!

I suddenly knew that I had shaken him off and gained my feet.

He rose, swaying. He was as tired, confused, as nearly asphyxiated as I.

The brink of the abyss was behind us. I lunged, desperately shoving, avoiding his clutch.

He went over, and fell soundlessly, his body whirling end over end down into the shadows, far below.

I drew back. My senses faded as I sank panting to the rocks. But with inactivity, my heart quieted. My respiration slowed. The Erentz circulation gained on my poisoned air. It purified.

That blessed oxygen! My head cleared. Strength came. I felt better.

Coniston had fallen to his death. I was victor. I went to the brink cautiously, for I was still dizzy. I could see, far down there on the crater floor, a little patch of Earthlight in which a mashed human figure was lying.

I staggered back again. A moment or two must have passed while I stood there on the summit, with my senses clearing and my strength renewed as the blood stream cleared in my veins.

I was victor. Coniston was dead. I saw now, down on the lower staircase below the camp ledge, another goggled figure lying huddled. That was Wilks, no doubt. Coniston had probably caught him there, surprised him, killed him.

My attention, as I stood gazing, went down to the camp buildings. Another figure was outside! It bounded along the ledge, reached the foot of the stairs at the top of which I was standing. With agile leaps, it came mounting at me!

Another brigand! Miko? No, it was not large enough to be Miko. I was still confused. I thought of Hahn. But that was absurd: Hahn was in the wreck of the *Planetara*. One of the stewards then....

The figure came up the staircase recklessly, to assail me. I took a step backward, bracing myself to receive this new antagonist. And then I looked further down and saw Miko! Unquestionably he, for there was no mistaking his giant figure. He was down on the camp ledge, running toward the foot of the stairs.

I thought of my revolver. I turned to try and find it. I was aware that the first of my assailants was at the stairhead. I swung back to see what this oncoming brigand was doing. He was on the summit: with a sailing leap he launched for me. I could have bounded away, but with a last look to locate the revolver, I braced myself for the shock.

The figure hit me. It was small and light in my clutching arms. I recall I saw that Miko was halfway up the stairs. I gripped my assailant. The audiphone contact brought a voice.

"Gregg, is it you?"

It was Anita!

XXVI

"Gregg, you're safe!"

She had heard the camp corridors resounding with the shouts that Wilks and Haljan were fighting. She had come upon a suit and helmet by the manual emergency lock, had run out through the lock, confused, with her only idea to stop Wilks and me from fighting. Then she had seen one of us killed. Impulsively, barely knowing what she was doing, she mounted the stairs, frantic to find if I were alive.

"Anita!"

Miko was coming fast! She had not seen him; for she had no thought of brigands - only the belief that either Wilks or I had been killed.

But now, as we stood together on the rocks near the observatory platform, I could see the towering figure of Miko nearing the top of the stairs.

"Anita, that's Miko! We must run!"

Then I saw my projector. It lay in a bowl-like depression quite near us. I jumped for it. And as I tore loose from Anita, she leaped down after me. It was a broken bowl in the rocks, some six feet deep. It was open on the side facing the stairs - a narrow, ravinelike gully, full of gray, broken, tumbled rock masses. The little gully was littered with crags and boulders.

But I could see out through it.

Miko had come to the head of the stairs. He stopped there, his great figure etched sharply by the Earthlight. I think he must have known that Coniston was the one who had fallen over the cliff, as my helmet and Coniston's were different enough for him to recognize which was which. He did not know who I was, but he did know me for an enemy.

He stood now at the summit, peering to see where we had gone. He was no more than fifty feet from us.

"Anita, lie down."

I pulled her down on the rocks. I took aim with my projector. But I had forgotten our helmet lights. Miko must have seen them just as I pulled the trigger. He jumped sidewise and dropped, but I could see him moving in the shadows to where a jutting rock gave him shelter. I fired, missing him again.

I had stood up to take aim. Anita pulled me sharply down beside her.

"Gregg, he's armed!"

It was his turn to fire. It came - the familiar vague flash of the paralyzing ray. It spat its tint of color on the rocks near us, but did not reach us.

A moment later, Miko bounded to another rock.

Time passed - only a few seconds. I could not see Miko momentarily. Perhaps he was crouching; perhaps he had moved away again. He was, or had been, on slightly higher ground than the bottom of our bowl. It was dim down here where we were lying, but I feared that any moment Miko might appear and strike at us. His ray at any short range would penetrate our visor panes, even though our suits might temporarily resist it.

"Anita, it's too dangerous here!"

Had I been alone, I might perhaps have leapt up to lure Miko. But with Anita I did not dare chance it.

"We've got to get back to camp," I told her.

"Perhaps he has gone -"

But he had not. We saw him again, out in a distant patch of Earthlight. He was further from us than before, but on still higher ground. We had extinguished our small helmet lights. But he knew we were here and possibly he could see us. His projector flashed again. He was a hundred feet or more away now, and his weapon was of no longer range than mine. I did not answer his fire, for I could not hope to hit him at such a distance, and the flash of my weapon would help him to locate us.

I murmured to Anita, "We must get away."

Yet how did I dare take Anita from these concealing shadows? Miko could reach us so easily as we bounded away in plain view in the Earthlight of the open summit! We were caught, at bay in this little bowl.

The camp was not visible from here. But out through the broken gully, a white beam of light suddenly came up from below.

Haljan. It spelled the signal.

It was coming from the Grantline instrument room, I knew.

I could answer it with my helmet light, but I did not dare.

"Try it," urged Anita.

We crouched where we thought we might be safe from Miko's

fire. My little light beam shot up from the bowl. It was undoubtedly visible to the camp.

Yes, I am Haljan. Send us help.

I did not mention Anita. Miko doubtless could read these signals. They answered, *Cannot -*

I lost the rest of it. There came a flash from Miko's weapon. It gave us confidence: he was unable to reach us at this distance.

The Grantline beam repeated:

Cannot come out. Ports broken. You cannot get in. Stay where you are for an hour or two. We may be able to repair ports.

I extinguished my light. What use was it to tell Grantline anything further? Besides, my light was endangering us. But the Grantline beam spelled another message:

Brigand ship is coming. It will be here before we can get out to you. No lights. We will try and hide our location.

And the signal beam brought a last appeal:

Miko and his men will divulge where we are unless you can stop them.

The beam vanished. The lights of the Grantline camp made a faint glow that showed above the crater edge. The glow died, as the camp now was plunged into darkness.

XXVII

We crouched in the shadows, the Earthlight filtering down to us. The skulking figure of Miko had vanished; but I was sure he was out there somewhere on the crags, lurking, maneuvering to where he could strike us with his ray. Anita's metal-gloved hand was on my arm; in my ear-diaphragm her voice sounded eager:

"What was the signal, Gregg?"

I told her everything.

"Oh Gregg! The Martian ship coming!"

Her mind clung to that as the most important thing. But not so myself. To me there was only the realization that Anita was caught out here, almost at the mercy of Miko's ray. Grantline's men could not get out to help us, nor could I get Anita into the camp.

She added, "Where do you suppose the ship is?"

"Twenty or thirty thousand miles up, probably."

The stars and the Earth were visible over us. Somewhere up there, disclosed by Grantline's instruments but not yet discernible to the naked eye, Miko's reinforcements were hovering.

We lay for a moment in silence. It was horribly nerve straining.

Miko could be creeping up on us. Would he dare chance my sudden fire? Creeping - or would he make a swift, unexpected rush?

The feeling that he was upon us abruptly swept me. I jumped to my feet, against Anita's effort to hold me. Where was he now? Was my imagination playing me tricks?...

I sank back. "That ship should be here in a few hours."

I told her what Grantline's signal had suggested; the ship was hovering overhead. It must be fairly close; for Grantline's telescope had revealed its identity as an outlaw flyer, unmarked by any of the standard code identification lights. It was doubtless too far away as yet to have located the whereabouts of Grantline's camp. The Martian brigands knew that we were in the vicinity of Archimedes, but no more than that. Searching this glowing Moon surface, our tiny local semaphore beams would certainly pass unnoticed.

But as the brigand ship approached now - dropping close to Archimedes as it probably would - our danger was that Miko and his men would then signal it, join it, and reveal the camp's location. And the brigand attack would be upon us!

I told this now to Anita. "The signal from Grantline said, '*Unless you can stop them.*'"

It was an appeal to me. But how could I stop them? What could I do, alone out here with Anita, to cope with this enemy?

Anita made no comment.

I added, "That ship will land near Archimedes, within an hour or two. If Grantline can repair the ports, and I can get you inside...."

Again she made no comment. Then suddenly she gripped me.

"Gregg, look there!"

Out through the gully break in our bowl the figure of Miko showed! He was running. But not at us. Circling the summit, leaping to keep himself behind the upstanding crags. He passed the head of the staircase; he did not descend it, but headed off along the summit of the crater rim.

I stood up to watch him. "Where's he going!"

I let Anita stand up beside me, cautiously at first, for it occurred to me it might be a ruse to cover some other of Miko's men who might be lurking near.

But the summit seemed clear. The figure of Miko was a thousand feet away now. We could see the tiny blob of it bobbing over the rocks. Then it plunged down - not into the crater valley, but out toward the open Moon surface.

Miko had abandoned his attack on us. The reason seemed plain. He had come here from his encampment with Coniston ahead to lure and kill Wilks. When this was done, Coniston had flashed his signal to Miko, who was hiding nearby.

It was not like the brigand leader to remain in the background. Miko was no coward. But Coniston could impersonate Wilks, whereas Miko's giant stature at once would reveal his identity. Miko had been engaged in smashing the ports. He had looked up and seen me kill Coniston. He had come to assail me. And then he had read Grantline's message to me. It was his first knowledge that his ship was at hand. With the camp exits inoperative, Grantline and his men were imprisoned. Miko had made an effort to kill me. He did not know my companion was Anita. But the effort was taking too long; with his ship at hand, it was Miko's best move to return to his own camp, rejoin his men, and await their opportunity to signal the ship.

At least, so I reasoned it. Anita and I stood alone. What could we do?

We went to the brink of the cliff. The unlighted Grantline buildings showed vaguely in the Earthlight.

I said, "We'll go down. I'll leave you there. You can wait at the port. They'll repair it soon."

"And what will you do, Gregg?"

I did not intend to tell her. "Hurry, Anita!"

"Gregg, let me go with you."

She jerked away from me and bounded back up the stairs. I caught her on the summit.

"Anita!"

"I'm going with you."

"You're going to stay here."

"I'm not!"

This exasperating controversy!

"Anita, please."

"I'll be safer with you than waiting here, Gregg." And she added, "Besides, I won't stay and you can't make me."

We ran along the crater top. At its distant edge the lower plain spread before us. Far down, and far away on the distant broken surface, the leaping figure of Miko showed. He plunged down the broken outer slope, reached the level. Soon, as we ran, the little Grantline crater faded behind us.

Anita ran more skillfully than I. Ten minutes or so passed. We had seen Miko and the direction he was taking, but down here on the plain we could no longer see him. It struck me that our chase was purposeless and dangerous. Suppose Miko were to see us following him? Suppose he stopped and lay in ambush to fire at us as we came leaping heedlessly by?

"Anita, wait!"

I drew her down amid a group of tumbled boulders. And then abruptly she clung to me.

"Gregg, I know what we can do! Gregg, don't tell me you won't let me try it!"

I listened to her plan. Incredible! Incredibly dangerous. Yet, as I pondered it, the very daring of the scheme seemed the measure of its possible success. The brigands would never imagine we could be so rash!

"But Anita -"

"Gregg, you're stupid!" It was her turn to be exasperated.

But I was in no mood for daring. My mind was obsessed with Anita's safety. I had been planning that we might see the glow of Miko's encampment and decide on some course of action.

"But, Gregg, the safety of the treasure - of all the Grantline men...."

"To the infernal with that! It's you, your safety -"

"My safety, then! If you put me in the camp and the brigands attack it and I am killed - what then? But this plan of mine, if we can do it, Gregg, will mean safety in the end for all of us."

And it seemed possible. We crouched, discussing it. So daring a thing!

The brigand ship would come down near Archimedes. That was fifty miles from Grantline. The brigands from Mars would not have seen the dark Grantline buildings hidden in the little crater pit. They would wait for Miko and his men to make their whereabouts known.

Miko's encampment was ahead of us now, undoubtedly. We had been following him toward the Mare Imbrium. Or at least, we hoped so. He would signal his ship. But Anita and I, closer to it, would also signal it; and, posing as brigands, would join it!

"Remember, Gregg, I remain Anita Prince, George's sister." Her voice trembled as she mentioned her dead brother. "They know that George was in Miko's pay, and I as his sister, will help to convince them."

This daring scheme! If we could join the ship, we might be able to persuade its leader that Miko's distant signals were merely a ruse of Grantline to lure the brigands in that direction. A long range projector from the ship would kill Miko and his men as they came forward to join it! And then we would falsely direct the brigands, lead them away from Grantline and the treasure.

"Gregg, we must try it."

Heaven help me, I yielded to her persuasion!

We turned at right angles and ran toward where the distant frowning walls of Archimedes loomed against the starlit sky.

XXVIII

The broken, shaggy ramparts of the giant crater rose above us. We toiled upward, out of the foothills, clinging now to the crags and pitted terraces of the main ascent. An hour had passed since we turned from the borders of Mare Imbrium. Or was it two hours? I could not tell. I only know that we ran with desperate, frantic haste.

Anita would not admit that she was tired. She was more skillful than I in this leaping over the broken rock masses. Yet I felt that her slight strength must give out. It seemed miles up the undulating slopes of the foothills with the black and white ramparts of the crater close before us.

And then the main ascent. There were places where, like smooth black frozen ice, the walls rose sheer. We avoided them, toiling aside, plunging into gullies, crossing pits where sometimes, perforce, we went downwards, and then up again. Or sometimes we stood, hot and breathless, upon ledges, recovering our strength, selecting the best route upward.

In tumbled mass of rock, honeycombed everywhere with caves and passages leading into impenetrable darkness, there were pits into which we might so easily have fallen; ravines to span, sometimes with a leap, sometimes by a long and arduous detour.

Endless climb. We came to the ledge with the plains of the Mare Imbrium stretching out beneath us. We might have been upon this main ascent for an hour; the plains were far down, the broken surface down there smoothed now by the perspective of height. And yet still above us the brooding circular wall went up into the sky. Ten thousand feet above us.

"You're tired, Anita. We'd better stay here."

"No. If we could only get to the top - the ship may land on the other side - they would see us."

There was as yet no sign of the brigand ship. With every stop for rest we searched the starry vault. The Earth hung over us, flattened beyond the full. The stars blazed to mingle with the Earthlight and illumine these massive crags of the Archimedes walls. But no speck appeared to tell us that the ship was up there.

We were on the curving side of the Archimedes wall which fronted the Mare Imbrium to the north. The plains lay Like a great frozen sea, congealed ripples shining in the light of the Earth, with dark patches to mark the hollows. Somewhere down there - six or eight thousand feet below us now - Miko's encampment lay concealed. We searched for lights of it, but could see none.

Had Miko rejoined his party, left his camp and come here like ourselves to climb Archimedes? Or was our assumption wholly wrong: perhaps the brigand ship would not land near here at all!

Sweeping around from the Mare Imbrium, the plains were less smooth. The little crater which concealed the Grantline camp was off in the crater-scarred region beyond which the distant Apennines raised their terraced walls. There was nothing to mark it from here.

"Gregg, do you see anything up there?" She added, "There seems to be a blur."

Her sight, sharper than mine, had picked it out. The descending brigand ship! A faintest, tiny blur against the stars, a few of them occulted as though an invisible shadow were upon them. A growing shadow, materializing into a blur - a blob, a shape faintly defined. Then sharper until we were sure of what we saw. It was the brigand ship. It was dropping slowly, silently down.

We crouched on the little ledge. A cave mouth was behind us. A gully was beside us, a break in the ledge; and at our feet the sheer wall dropped.

We had extinguished our lights. We crouched, silently gazing up into the stars.

The ship, when we first distinguished it, was centered over Archimedes. We thought for a while that it might descend into the crater. But it did not; it came sailing forward.

I whispered into the audiphone, "It's coming over the crater."

Her hand pressed my arm in answer.

I recalled that when, from the *Planetara*, Miko had forced Snap to signal this brigand band on Mars, Miko's only information as to the whereabouts of the Grantline camp was that it lay between Archimedes and the Apennines. The brigands now were following that information.

A tense interval passed. We could see the ship plainly above us now, a gray-black shape among the stars up beyond the shaggy, towering crater rim. The vessel came upon a level keel, hull down. Slowly circling,
looking for Miko's signal, no doubt, or for possible lights from Grantline's camp. They might also be picking a landing place.

We saw it soon as a cylindrical, cigarlike shape, rather smaller than the *Planetara*, but similar of design. It bore lights now. The ports of its hull were tiny rows of illumination, and the glow of light under its rounding upper dome was faintly visible.

A bandit ship, no doubt of that. Its identification keel plate was empty of official pass code lights. These brigands had not attempted to secure official sailing lights when leaving Ferrok-Shahn. It was unmistakably an outlaw ship. And here upon the deserted Moon there was no need for secrecy. Its lights were openly displayed, that Miko might see it and join it.

It went slowly past us, only a few thousand feet higher than our level. We could see the whole outline of its pointed cylinder hull, with the rounded dome on top. And under the dome was its open deck with a little cabin superstructure in the center.

I thought for a moment that by some unfortunate chance it might land quite near us. But it went past. And then I saw that it was heading for a level, plateaulike surface a few miles further on. It dropped, cautiously floating down.

There was still no sign of Miko. But I realized that haste was necessary. We must be the first to join the brigand ship.

I lifted Anita to her feet. "I don't think we should signal from here."

"No. Miko might see it."

We could not tell where he was. Down on the plains, perhaps? Or up here, somewhere in these miles of towering rocks?

"Are you ready, Anita?"

"Yes, Gregg."

I stared through the visors at her white solemn face.

"Yes, I'm ready," she repeated.

Her hand pressure seemed to me suddenly like a farewell. We were plunging rashly into what was destined to mean our death? Was this a farewell?

An instinct told me not to do this thing. Why, in a few hours I could have Anita back to the comparative safety of the Grantline camp. The exit ports would doubtless be repaired by now. I could get her inside.

She had bounded away from me, leaped down some thirty feet into the broken gully, to cross it and then up on the other side. I stood for an instant watching her fantastic shape, with the great rounded, goggled, trunked helmet and the lump on her shoulders which held the little Erentz motors. Then I hurried after her.

It did not take us long - two or three miles of circling along the giant wall. The ship lay only a few hundred feet above our level.

We stood at last on a buttelike pinnacle. The lights of the ship were close over us. And there were moving lights up there, tiny moving spots on the adjacent rocks. The brigands had come out, prowling about to investigate their location.

No signal yet from Miko. But it might come at any moment.

"I'll flash now," I whispered.

"Yes."

The brigands had probably not yet seen us. I took the lamp from my helmet. My hand was trembling. Suppose my signal were answered by a shot? A flash from some giant projector mounted on the ship?

Anita crouched behind a rock, as she had promised. I stood with my torch and flung its switch. My puny light beam shot up. I waved it, touched the ship with its faint glowing circle of illumination.

They saw me. There was a sudden movement among the lights up there.

I semaphored:

I am from Miko. Do not fire.

I used open universal code. In Martian first, and then in English.

There was no answer, but no attack. I tried again.

This is Haljan, one of the Planetara. *George Prince's sister is with me. There has been disaster to Miko.*

A small light beam came down from the brink of the overhead cliff beside the ship.

Continue.

I went steadily on: *Disaster - the* Planetara *is wrecked. All killed but me and Prince's sister. We want to join you.*

I flashed off my light. The answer came:

Where is the Grantline Camp?

Near here. The Mare Imbrium.

As though to answer my lie, from down on the Earthlit plains, some ten miles or so from the crater base, a tiny signal light shot up. Anita saw it and gripped me.

"There is Miko's light!"

It spelled in Martian, *Come down. Land Mare Imbrium.*

Miko had seen the signaling up here and had joined it! He repeated, *Land Mare Imbrium.*

I flashed a protest up to the ship: *Beware. That is Grantline! Trickery.*

From the ship the summons came, *Come up.*

We had won this first encounter! Miko must have realized his disadvantage. His distant light went out.

"Come, Anita."

There was no retreat now. But again I seemed to feel in the pressure of her hand that vague farewell. Her voice whispered, "We must do our best, act our best to be convincing."

In the white glow of a searchbeam we climbed the crags, reached the broad upper ledge. Helmeted figures rushed at us, searched us for weapons, seized our helmet lights. The evil face of a giant Martian peered at me through the visors. Two other monstrous, towering figures seized Anita.

We were shoved toward the port locks at the base of the ship's hull. Above the hull bulge I could see the grids of projectors mounted on the dome side, and the figures of men standing on the deck, peering down at us.

We went through the admission locks into a hull corridor, up an incline passage, and reached the lighted deck. The Martian brigands crowded around us.

XXIX

Anita's words echoed in my memory: "We must do our best to be convincing." It was not her ability that I doubted, as much as my own. She had played the part of George Prince cleverly, unmasked only by an evil chance.

I steeled myself to face the searching glances of the brigands as they shoved around us. This was a desperate game into which we had plunged. For all our acting, how easy it would be for some small chance thing abruptly to undo us! I realized it, and now, as I gazed into the peering faces of these men from Mars, I cursed myself for the witless rashness which had brought Anita into this!

The brigands - some ten or fifteen of them here on deck - stood in a ring around us. They were all big men, nearly of a seven-foot average, dressed in leather jerkins and short leather breeches, with bare knees and flaring leather boots. Piratical swaggering fellows, knife-blades mingled with small hand projectors fastened to their belts. Gray, heavy faces, some with scraggly, unshaven beards. They plucked at us, jabbering in Martian.

One of them seemed the leader. I said sharply, "Are you the commander here? You speak the Earth English?"

"Yes," he said readily. "I am commander here." He spoke English with the same freedom and accent as Miko. "Is this George Prince's sister?"

"Yes. Her name is Anita Prince. Tell your men to take their hands off her."

He waved his men away. They all seemed more interested in Anita than in me. He added:

"I am *Set* Potan." He addressed Anita. "George Prince's sister? You are called Anita? I have heard of you. I knew your brother - indeed, you look very much like him."

He swept his plumed hat to the grid with a swaggering gesture of homage. A courtierlike fellow this, debonair as a Venus cavalier!

He accepted us. I realized that Anita's presence was extremely valuable in making us convincing. Yet there was about this Potan - as with Miko - a disturbing suggestion of irony. I could not make him out. I decided that we had fooled him. Then I remarked the steely glitter of his eyes as he turned to me.

"You were an officer of the *Planetara*?"

The insignia of my rank was visible on my white jacket collar which showed beneath the Erentz suit now that my helmet was off.

"Yes. I was supposed to be. But a year ago I embarked upon this adventure with Miko."

He was leading us to his cabin. "The *Planetara* wrecked? Miko dead?"

"And Hahn and Coniston. George Prince too. We are the only survivors."

While we divested ourselves of the Erentz suits, at his command, I told him briefly of the *Planetara's* fall. All had been killed on board, save Anita and me. We had escaped, awaited his coming. The treasure was here; we had located the Grantline camp, and were ready to lead him to it.

Did he believe me? He listened quietly. He seemed not shocked at the death of his comrades. Nor yet pleased: merely imperturbable.

I added with a sly, sidelong glance, "There were too many of us on the *Planetara*. The purser had joined us and many of the crew. And there was Miko's sister, the *Setta* Moa - too many. The treasure divides better among less."

An amused smile played on his thin gray lips. But he nodded. The fear which had leaped at me was allayed by his next words.

"True enough, Haljan. He was a domineering fellow, Miko. A third of it all was for him alone. But now...."

The third would go to this sub-leader, Potan! The implication was obvious.

I said, "Before we go any further, I can trust you for my share?"

"Of course."

I figured that my very boldness in bargaining so prematurely would convince him. I insisted, "Miss Prince will have her brother's share?"

Clever Anita! She put in swiftly, "Oh, I give no information until you promise! We know the location of the Grantline camp, its weapons, its defences, the amount and location of the treasure. I warn you, if you do not play us fair...."

He laughed heartily. He seemed to like us. He spread his huge legs as he lounged in his settle, and drank of the bowl which one of his men set before him.

"Little tigress! Fear me not - I play fair!" He pushed two of the bowls across the table. "Drink, Haljan. All is well with us and I am glad to know it. Miss Prince, drink my health as your leader."

I waved it away from Anita. "We need all our wits; your strong Martian drinks are dangerous. Look here, I'll tell you just how the situation stands -"

I plunged into a glib account of our supposed wanderings to find the Grantline camp: its location off the Mare Imbrium - hidden in a cavern there. Potan, with the drink, and under the gaze of Anita's eyes, was in high good humor. He laughed when I told him that we had dared to invade the Grantline camp, had smashed its exit ports, had even gotten up to have a look where the treasure was piled.

"Well done, Haljan. You're a fellow to my liking!" But his gaze was on Anita. "You dress like a man or a charming boy."

She still wore the dark clothes of her brother. She said, "I am used to action. Man's garb pleases me. You shall treat me like a man and give me my share of gold leaf."

He had already demanded the reason for the signal from the Mare Imbrium. Miko's signal! It had not come again, though any moment I feared it. I told him that Grantline doubtless had repaired his damaged ports and sallied out to assail me in reprisal. And, seeing the brigand ship landing on Archimedes, had tried to lure him into a trap.

I wondered if my explanation was convincing: it did not sound so. But he was flushed now with drink, and Anita added:

"Grantline knows the territory near his camp very well. But he is equipped only for short range fighting."

I took it up. "It's like this, Potan: if he could get you to land unsuspectingly near his cavern -"

I pictured how Grantline might have figured on a sudden surprise attack upon the ship. It was his only chance to catch it unprepared.

We were all three in friendly, intimate mood now. Potan said, "We'll land down there right enough! But I need a few hours for my assembling."

"He will not dare advance," I said.

Anita put in, smiling, "He knows by now that we have unmasked his lure. Haljan and I, joining you - that silenced him. His light went out very promptly, didn't it?"

She flashed me a side gaze. Were we acting convincingly? But if Miko started up his signals again, they might so quickly betray us! Anita's thoughts were upon that, for she added:

"Grantline will not dare show his light! If he does, *Set* Potan, we can blast him from here with a ray. Can't we?"

"Yes," Potan agreed. "If he comes within ten miles, I have one powerful enough. We are assembling it now."

"And we have thirty men?" Anita persisted. "When we sail down to attack him, it should not be difficult to kill all the Grantline party."

"By heaven, Haljan, this girl of yours is small, but very bloodthirsty!"

"And I'm glad Miko is dead," Anita added.

I explained, "That accursed Miko murdered her brother."

Acting! And never once did we dare relax. If only Miko's signals would hold off and give us time!

* * * * *

We may have talked for half an hour. We were in a small steel-lined cubby, located in the forward deck of the ship. The dome was over it. I could see from where I sat at the table that there was a forward observatory tower under the dome quite near here. The ship was laid out in rather similar fashion to the *Planetara*, though considerably smaller.

Potan had dismissed his men from the cubby so as to be alone with us. Out on the deck I could see them dragging apparatus about, bringing the mechanisms of giant projectors up from below and beginning to assemble them. Occasionally some of the men would come to our cubby windows to peer in curiously.

My mind was roaming as I talked. For all my manner of casualness, I knew that haste was necessary. Whatever Anita and I were to do must be quickly done.

But to win this fellow's utter confidence first was necessary, so that we might have the freedom of the ship, might move about unnoticed, unwatched.

I was horribly tense inside. Through the dome windows across the deck from the cubby, the rocks of the Lunar landscape were visible. I could see the brink of this ledge upon which the ship lay, the descending crags down the precipitous wall of Archimedes to the Earthlit plains far below. Miko, Moa, and a few of the *Planetara's* crew were down there somewhere.

Anita and I had a fairly definite plan. We were now in Potan's confidence; this interview at an end, I felt that our status among the brigands would be established. We would be free to move about the ship, join in its activities. It ought to be possible to locate the signal room, get friendly with the operator there.

Perhaps we could find a secret opportunity to flash a signal to Earth. This ship, I was confident, would have the power for a long range signal, if not of too sustained a length. It would be a desperate thing to attempt, but our whole procedure was desperate! Anita could lure the duty man from the signal room, I might send a single flash or two that would reach the Earth. Just a distress signal, signed "Grantline." If I could do that and not get caught!

Anita was engaging Potan in talking of his plans. The brigand leader was boasting of them: of his well equipped ship, the daring of his men. And questioning her about the size of the treasure. My thoughts were free to roam.

While we were making friends with this brigand, the longest range electronic projector was being assembled. Miko then could flash his signal and be damned to him! I would be on the deck with that projector. Its operator and I would turn it upon Miko - one flash of it and he and his little band would be wiped out.

But there was our escape to be thought of. We could not remain very long with these brigands. We could tell them that the Grantline camp was on the Mare Imbrium. It would delay them for a time, but our lie would soon be discovered. We must escape from them, get away and back to Grantline. With Miko dead, a distress signal to Earth, and Potan in ignorance of Grantline's location, the treasure would be safe until help arrived from Earth.

"By the infernal, little Anita, you look like a dove, but you're a tigress! A comrade after my own heart - bloodthirsty as a fire-worshipper!"

Her laugh rang out to mingle with his. "Oh no, *Set* Potan! I am treasure-thirsty."

"We'll get the treasure. Never fear, little Anita."

"With you to lead us, I'm sure we will."

A man entered the cubby. Potan looked frowningly around.

"What is it, Argle?"

The fellow answered in Martian, leered at Anita and withdrew.

Potan stood up. I noticed that he was unsteady with the drink.

"They want me with the work at the projectors."

"Go ahead," I said.

He nodded. We were comrades now. "Amuse yourself, Haljan. Or come out on deck if you wish. I will tell my men you are one of us."

"And tell them to keep their hands off Miss Prince."

He stared at me. "I had not thought of that: a woman among so many men!"

His own gaze at Anita was as offensive as any of his men could have given. He said, "Have no fear, little tigress."

Anita laughed. "I'm afraid of nothing."

But when he had lurched from the cabin, she touched me. Smiled with her mannish swagger, for fear we were still observed, and murmured:

"Oh Gregg, I am afraid!"

We stayed in the cubby a few moments, whispering and planning.

"You think the signal room is in the tower, Gregg? This tower outside our window here?"

"Yes, I think so."

"Shall we go out and see?"

"Yes. Keep near me always."

"Oh Gregg, I will!"

We deposited our Erentz suits carefully in a corner of the cubby. We might need them so suddenly! Then we swaggered out to join the brigands working on the deck.

XXX

The deck glowed lurid in the queer blue-greenish glare of Martian electro-fuse lights. It was in a bustle of ordered activity. Some twenty of the crew were scattered about, working in little groups. Apparatus was being brought up from below to be assembled. There was a pile of Erentz suits and helmets, of Martian pattern, but still very similar to those with which Grantline's expedition was equipped. There were giant projectors of several kinds, some familiar to me, others of a fashion I had never seen before. It seemed there were six or eight of them, still dismantled, with a litter of their attendant batteries and coils and tube amplifiers.

They were to be mounted here on the deck, I surmised; I saw in the dome side one or two of them already rolled into position.

Anita and I stood outside Potan's cubby, gazing around us curiously. The men looked at us but none of them spoke.

"Let's watch from here a moment," I whispered. She nodded, standing with her hand on my arm. I felt that we were very small, here in the midst of these seven foot Martian men. I was all in white, the costume used in the warm interior of Grantline's camp. Bareheaded, white silk *Planetara* uniform jacket, broad belt and tight-laced trousers. Anita was a slim black figure beside me, somber as Hamlet, with her pale boyish face and wavy black hair.

The gravity being maintained here on the ship we had found to be stronger than that of the Moon and rather more like Mars.

"There are the heat rays, Gregg."

A pile of them was visible down the deck length. And I saw caskets of fragile glass globes, bombs of different styles, hand projectors of the paralyzing ray; search beams of several varieties; the Benson curve light, and a few side arms of ancient Earth design - swords and dirks, and small bullet projectors.

There seemed to be some mining equipment also. Far along the deck, beyond the central cabin in the open space of the stern, steel rails were stacked; half a dozen tiny-wheeled ore carts; a tiny motor engine for hauling them and what looked as though it might be the dismembered sections of an ore chute.

The whole deck was presently strewn with this mass of equipment.

Potan moved about, directing the different groups of workers. The news had spread that we knew the location of the treasure. The brigands were jubilant. In a few hours the ship's armament would be ready, and it would advance.

I saw many glances cast out the dome side windows toward the distant plains of the Mare Imbrium. The brigands believed that the Grantline camp lay in that direction.

Anita whispered, "Which is their giant electronic projector, Gregg?"

I could see it amidships of the deck. It was already in place. Potan was there now, superintending the men who were connecting it. The most powerful weapon on the ship. It had, Potan said, an effective range of some ten miles. I wondered what it would do to a Grantline building! The Erentz double walls would withstand it for a time, I was sure. But it would blast an Erentz fabric suit, no doubt of that. Like a lightning bolt, it would kill - its flashing free stream of electrons shocking the heart, bringing instant death.

I whispered, "We must smash that before we leave! But first turn it on Miko, if he signals now."

I was tensely watchful for that signal. The electronic projector obviously was not ready. But when it was connected, I must be near it, to persuade its duty man to fire it on Miko. With this done we would have more time to plan our other tasks. I did not think Potan would be ready for his attack before another time of sleep here in the ship's routine. Things would be quieter then; I would watch my chance to send a signal to Earth, and then we would escape.

With my thoughts roving, we had been standing quietly at the cubby door for about fifteen minutes. My hand in my side pouch clutched the little bullet projector. The brigands had taken it from me and given it to Potan. He had placed it on the settle with my Erentz suit; and when we gained his confidence he had forgotten it and left it there. I had it now, and the feel of its cool sleek handle gave me a measure of comfort. Things could go wrong so easily. But if they did, I was determined to sell my life as dearly as possible. And a vague thought was in my mind: I must not use the last bullet. That would be for Anita.

"That electronic projector is remote controlled. Look, Anita, that's the signal room over us. The giant projector will be aimed and fired from up there."

A thirty foot skeleton tower stood on the deck near us, with a spiral ladder leading up to a small, square, steel cubby at the top. Through the cubby window I could see instrument panels. A single Martian was up there; he had called down to Potan concerning the electronic projector.

The roof of this little tower room was close under the dome - a space of no more than four feet. A pressure lock exit in the dome was up there, with a few steps leading up to it from the roof of the tower signal room.

We could escape that way, perhaps. In the event of dire necessity it might be possible. But only as a desperate resort, for it would put us on the top of the glassite dome, with a sheer hundred feet or more down its sleek bulging exterior side, and down the outside bulge of the ship's hull, to the rocks below. There might be a spider ladder outside leading downward, but I saw no evidence of it. If Anita and I were forced to escape that way, I wondered how we could manage a hundred foot jump to the rocks, and land safely. Even with the slight gravity of the Moon, it would be a dangerous fall.

"You are Gregg Haljan?"

I stared as one of the brigands, coming up behind, addressed me.

"Yes."

"Commander Potan tells me you were chief navigator of the *Planetara*?"

"Yes."

"You shall pilot us when we advance upon the Grantline camp. I am control-commander here - Brotow, my name."

He smiled. A giant fellow, but spindly. He spoke good English. He seemed anxious to be friendly.

"We are glad to have you and George Prince's sister with us." He shot Anita an admiring glance. "I will show you our controls, Haljan."

"All right," I said. "Whatever I can do to help...."

"But not now. It will be some hours before we are ready."

I nodded, and he wandered away. Anita whispered: "Did he mean that signal room up in the tower? Oh Gregg, maybe it's only the control room."

"Suppose we go up and see? Miko's signals might start any minute."

And the electronic projector seemed about ready. It was time for me to act. But a reluctant instinct was upon me. Our Erentz suits were close behind us in Potan's cubby. I hated to leave them. If anything happened, and we had to make a sudden dash, there would be no time to garb ourselves in the suits. To adjust the helmets would be bad enough.

I whispered swiftly, "We must get into our suits - find some pretext." I drew her back through the cubby doorway where we would be more secluded.

"Anita, listen. I've been a fool not to plan our escape more carefully. We're in too great a danger here!"

Suddenly it seemed to me that we were in desperate plight! Was it premonition?

"Anita, listen: if anything happens and we have to make a dash -"

"Up through that dome lock, Gregg? It's a manual control; you can see the levers."

"Yes. It's a manual. But once up there how would we get down?"

She was far calmer than I. "There may be an outside ladder, Gregg."

"I don't think so. I haven't seen it."

"Then we can get out the way they brought us in. The hull port - it's a manual, too."

"Yes, I think I can find our way down through the hull corridors."

"There are guards outside on the rocks."

We had seen them through the dome windows. But there were not many, only two or three. I was armed and a surprise rush would do the trick.

We donned our Erentz suits.

"What will we do with the helmets?" demanded Anita. "Leave them here?"

"No, take them with us. I'm not going to get separated from them!"

"We'll look strange going up to that signal room equipped like this."

"I can't help it, Anita. We'll explain it, somehow."

She stood before me, a queer-looking little figure in the now deflated, bagging suit with her slim neck and head protruding above it.

"Carry your helmet, Anita. Ill take mine."

We could adjust the helmets and start the motors all within a few seconds.

"I'm ready, Gregg."

"Come on, then. Let me go first."

I had the bullet projector in an outer pouch of the suit where I could instantly reach it. This was more rational; we had a fighting chance now. The fear which had swept me began to recede.

"We'll climb the tower to the signal room," I whispered. "Do it boldly."

We stepped from the cubby. Potan was not in sight; perhaps he was on the further deck beyond the central cabin structure.

On the deck, we were immediately accosted. This was different - our appearance in the Erentz suits!

"Where are you going?" This fellow spoke in Martian.

I answered in English, "Up there."

He stood before us, towering over me. I saw a group of nearby workers stop to regard us. In a moment we would be causing a commotion, and it was the last thing I desired.

I said in Martian, "Commander Potan told me, what I wish I can do. From the dome we look around to see where is the Grantline camp from here. I am pilot of this ship to go there."

The man who had called himself Brotow passed near us. I appealed to him.

"We put on our suits. After our experience, we feel safer that way. If I'm to pilot the ship...."

He hesitated, his glance sweeping the deck as though to ask Potan. Someone said in Martian:

"The Commander is down in the stern storeroom."

It decided Brotow. He waved away the Martian who had stopped me.

"Let them pass."

Anita and I gave him our most friendly smiles.

"Thanks."

He bowed to Anita with a sweeping gesture. "I will show you over the control room presently."

His gaze went to the peak of the bow.

The little hooded cubby there was the control room, then. Satisfaction swept me. Then above us in the tower, must surely be the signal room. Would Brotow follow us up? I hoped not. I wanted to be alone with the duty man up there, giving me a chance to get at the projector controls if Miko's signal should come.

I drew Anita past Brotow, who had stood aside. "Thanks," I repeated. "We won't be long."

We mounted the little ladder.

XXXI

"Hurry, Anita!"

I feared that Potan might come up from the hull at any moment and stop us. The duty man over us gazed down, his huge head and shoulders blocking the small signal room window. Brotow called up in Martian, telling him to let us come. He scowled, but when we reached the trap in the room floor grid, we found him standing aside to admit us.

I flung a swift glance around. It was a metallic cubby, not much over fifteen feet square, with an eight foot arched ceiling. There were instrument panels. The range finder for the giant projector was here; its telescope with the trajectory apparatus and the firing switch were unmistakable. And the signaling apparatus was here! Not a Martian set, but a fully powerful Botz ultra-violet sender with its attendant receiving mirrors. The *Planetara* had used the Botz system, so I was thoroughly familiar with it.

I saw too, what seemed to be weapons: a row of small fragile glass globes, hanging on clips along the wall - bombs, each the size of a man's fist. And a broad belt with bombs in its padded compartments.

My heart was pounding as my first quick glance took in these details. I saw also that the room had four small oval window openings. They were breast high above the floor; from the deck below I knew that the angle of vision was such that the men down there could not see into this room except to glimpse its upper portion near the ceiling. And the helio set was banked on a low table near the floor.

In a corner of the room a small ladder led through a ceiling trap to the cubby roof. This upper trap was open. Four feet above the room's roof was the arch of the dome, with the entrance to the exit-lock directly above us. The weapons and the belt of bombs were near the ascending ladder, evidently placed here as equipment for use from the top of the dome.

I turned to the solitary duty man. I must gain his confidence at once. Anita had laid her helmet aside. She spoke first.

"We were with *Set* Miko," she said smilingly, "in the wreck of the *Planetara*. You heard of it? We know where the treasure is."

This duty man was a full seven feet tall, and the most heavy-set Martian I had ever seen. A tremendous, beetle-browed, scowling fellow. He stood with hands on his hips, his leather-garbed legs spread wide; and as I confronted him, I felt like a child.

He was silent, glaring down at me as I drew his attention from Anita.

"You speak English?" I asked. "We are not skilled with Martian."

I wondered if at the next time of sleep this fellow would be on duty here. I hoped not: it would not be easy to trick him and find an opportunity to flash a signal. But that task was some hours away as yet; I would worry about it when the time came. Just now I was concerned with Miko and his little band, who at any moment might arrive in sight. If we could persuade this duty man to turn the projector on them!

He answered me in ready English:

"You are the man Gregg Haljan? And this is the sister of George Prince - what do you want up here?"

"I am a navigator. Brotow wants me to pilot the ship when we advance to attack Grantline."

"This is not the control room."

"No, I know it isn't."

I put my helmet carefully on the floor beside Anita's. I straightened to find the brigand gazing at her. He did not speak: he was still scowling. But in the dim blue glow of the cubby, I caught the look in his eyes.

I said hastily, "Grantline knows your ship has landed here on Archimedes. His camp is off there on the Mare Imbrium. He sent up a signal - you saw it, didn't you? - just before Miss Prince and I came aboard. He was trying to pretend he was your Earth party, Miko and Coniston."

"Why?"

The fellow turned his scowl on me, but Anita brought his gaze back to her. She put in quickly:

"Grantline, as brother always said, has no great cunning. I believe now he plans to creep up on us unawares, by pretending that he is Miko."

"If he does that," I said, "we will turn this electronic projector on him and his party and annihilate them. You have its firing mechanism here."

"Who told you so?" he shot at me.

I gestured. "I see it here. It's obvious: I'm skilled at trajectory firing. If Grantline appears down there now, I'll help you."

"Is it connected?" Anita demanded boldly.

"Yes," he said. "You have on your Erentz suits: are you going to the dome roof? Then go."

But that was what we did not want to do. Anita's glance seemed to tell me to let her handle this. I turned toward one of the cubby windows.

She said sweetly, "Are you in charge of this room? Show me how the projector is operated. I know it will be invincible against the Grantline camp."

I had my back to them for a moment. Through the breast-high oval I could see down across the deck-space and out through the side dome windows. And my heart suddenly leaped into my throat. It seemed that down there in the Earthlit shadows, where the spreading base of the giant crater joined the plains, a light was bobbing. I gazed, stricken. Miko's lights? Was he advancing, preparing to signal? I tried to gauge the distance; it was not over two miles from here.

Or was it not a light at all? With the naked eye, I could not be sure. Perhaps there was a telescope finder here in the cubby....

I was subconsciously aware of the voices of Anita and the duty man behind me. Then abruptly I heard Anita's low cry. I whirled around.

The giant Martian had gathered her into his huge arms, his heavy jowled gray face, with a leering grin, close to hers!

He saw me coming. He held her with one arm! his other flung at me, caught me, knocked me backward. He rasped:

"Get out of here! Go up to the dome -"

Anita was silently struggling with her little hands at his thick throat. His blow flung me against a settle. But I held my feet. I was partly behind him. I leaped again, and as he tried to disengage himself from Anita to front me, her clutching fingers impeded him.

My projector was in my hand. But in that second as I leaped, I had the sense to realize I should not fire it because its noise would alarm the ship. I grasped its barrel, reached upward and struck with its heavy metal butt. The blow caught the Martian on the skull, and simultaneously my body struck him.

We went down together, falling partly upon Anita. But the giant had not cried out, and as I gripped him now, I felt his body go limp. I lay panting. Anita squirmed silently from under us. Blood from the giant's head was welling out, hot and sticky against my face as I lay sprawled on him.

I cast him off. He was dead, his fragile Martian skull split open by my blow.

There had been no alarm. The slight noise we made had not been heard down on the busy deck. Anita and I crouched by the floor. From the deck all this part of the room could not be seen.

"Dead."

"Oh Gregg -"

It forced our hand. I could not wait now for Miko to come. But I could flash the Earth signal now, and then we would have to make our run to escape.

Then I remembered that light down by the base! I kept Anita out of sight down on the floor and went cautiously to a window. The deck was in turmoil with brigands moving about excitedly. Not because of what had happened in our tower signal room: they were unaware of that.

Miko's signals were showing! I could see them now plainly,

down at the crater base. A group of hand lights and small waving helio beam.

And they were being answered from the ship! Potan was on the deck - a babble of voices, above which his rose with roars of command. At one of the dome windows a brigand with a hand searchbeam was sending its answering light. And I saw that Potan was working over a deck telescope finder.

It had all come so suddenly that I was stunned. But I did not wait to read the signals. I swung back at Anita, who stared helplessly at me.

"It's Miko! And they are answering him! Get your helmet: I'll try firing the projector."

Or would I instead try and send a brief flash signal to Earth? There would be no time to do both: we must escape out of here. The route up through the dome was the only feasible one now.

This range mechanism of the projector was reasonably familiar, and I felt that I could operate it. The range-finder and the switch were on a ledge at one of the windows. I rushed to it. As I swung the telescope, training it down on Miko's lights, I could see the huge projector on the deck swinging similarly. Its movement surprised the men who were attending it. One of them called up to me, but I ignored him.

Then Potan looked up and saw me. He shouted in Martian at the duty man, whom he doubtless thought was behind me: "Be ready! We may fire on them. I'll give you the word."

The signals were proceeding. It had only been a moment. I caught something like, "*Haljan is imposter.*"

I was aiming the projector. I was aware of Anita at my elbow. I pushed her back.

"Put on your helmet!"

I had the range. I flung the firing switch.

At the deck window the giant projector spat its deadly electronic stream. The men down there leaped away from it in surprise. I heard Potan's voice, his shout of protest and anger.

But down in the Earth glow at the crater base, Miko's lights had not vanished! I had missed! An error in the range? Abruptly I knew it was not that. Miko's lights were still there. His signals still coming. And I noticed now a faint distortion about them, the glow of his little group of hand lights faintly distorted and vaguely shot with a greenish cast. Benson curve lights!

My thoughts whirled in the few seconds while I stood there at the tower window. Miko had feared he might be summarily fired on. He had gone back to his camp, equipped all his lights with the Benson curve. He was somewhere at the crater base now. But not where I thought I saw him! The Benson curve light changed the path of the light rays traveling from him to me, I could not even approximate his true position!

Anita was plucking at me. "Gregg, come."

"I can't hit him," I gasped.

Should I try the flash signal to Earth? Did we dare linger here? I stood another few seconds at the window. I saw Potan down in the confusion of the deck, training a telescope. He had shouted up violently at his duty man here not to fire again.

And now he let out a roar. "I can see them! It's Miko! By the Almighty - his giant stature - Brotow, look! That's not an Earth man!"

He flung aside his telescope finder. "Disconnect that projector! It's Miko down there! This Haljan is a trickster! Where is he?

Braile - Braile, you accursed fool! Are Haljan and the girl up there with you?"

But the duty man lay in his blood at our feet.

I had dropped back from the window. Anita and I crouched for an instant in confusion, fumbling with our helmets.

The ship rang with the alarm. And amid the turmoil we could hear the shouts of the infuriated brigands swarming up the tower ladder after us!

XXXII

I was only inactive a moment. I had thought Anita would have on her helmet. But she was reluctant, or confused.

"Anita, we've got to get out of here! Up through the overhead locks to the dome."

"Yes." She fumbled with her helmet. The climbing men on the ladder were audible. They were already nearing the top. The trap door was closed; Anita and I were crouching on it. There was a thick metal bar set in a depressed groove for the grid. I slid it in place; it would seal the trap for a short time.

A degree of confidence came to me. We had a few moments before there could be any hand-to-hand conflict. The giant electronic projector would eventually be used against Grantline; it was the brigands' most powerful weapon. Its controls were here, by Heaven, I would smash them? That at least I could do!

I jumped for the window. Miko's signals had stopped, but I caught a glimpse of his distant moving curve lights.

A flash came up at me, as in the window I became visible to the brigands on the ship's deck. It was a small hand projector, hastily fired, for it went wide of the window. It was followed by a rain of small beams, but I was warned and dropped my head beneath the sill. The rays flashed dangerously upward through the oval opening, hissed against our vaulted roof. The air snapped and tingled with a shower of blue-red sparks, and the acrid odor of the released gases settled down upon us.

The trajectory controls of the projector were beside me. I seized them, ripped and tore at them. There was a roar down on the deck. The projector had exploded. A man's agonizing scream split the confusion of sounds.

It silenced the brigands on the deck. Under our floor grid, those on the ladder had been pounding at the trap door. They stopped, evidently to see what had happened. The bombardment of our windows stopped momentarily.

I cautiously peered out the window again. In the wreck of the projector, three men were lying. One of them was screaming horribly. The dome side was damaged. Potan and other men were frantically investigating to see if the ship's air was hissing out.

A triumph swept over me. They had not found me so meek and inoffensive as they might have thought!

Anita clutched me. She still had not donned her helmet.

"Put on your helmet!"

"But Gregg -"

"Put it on!"

"I.... I don't want to put it on until you put yours on."

"I've smashed the projector! We've stopped them coming up for a while."

But they were still on the ladder under our floor. They heard our voices: they began thumping again. Then pounding. They seemed now to have heavy implements. They rammed against the trap.

The floor seemed holding. The square of metal grid trembled, yielded a little. But it was good for a few minutes longer.

I called down, "The first one who comes through will be shot!" My words mingled with their oaths. There was a moment's pause, then the ramming went on. The dying man on the deck was still screaming.

I whispered, "I'll try an Earth signal."

She nodded. Pale, tense, but calm. "Yes, Gregg. And I was thinking -"

"It won't take a minute. Have your helmet ready."

"I was thinking -" She hurried across the room.

I swung on the Botz signaling apparatus. It was connected. Within a moment I had it humming. The fluorescent tubes lighted with their lurid glare; they painted purple the body of the giant duty man who lay sprawled at my feet. I drew on all the ship's power. The tube lights in the room quivered and went dim.

I would have to hurry. Potan could shut this off from the main hull control room. I could see, through the room's upper trap, the primary sending mirror mounted in the peak of the dome. It was quivering, radiant with its light energy. I sent the flash.

The flattened past full Earth was up there. I knew that the Western Hemisphere faced the Moon at this hour. I flashed in English, with the open Universal Earth code:

Help. Grantline.

And again: *Help. Archimedes region near Apennines. Attacked by brigands.*

Send help at once. Grantline.

If only it would be received! I flung off the current. Anita stood watching me intently. "Gregg, look!"

I saw that she had taken some of the glass globe-bombs which lay by the foot of the ascending ladder. "Gregg, I threw some of them."

At the window we gazed down. The globes she flung had shattered on the deck. They were darkness bombs.

Through the blackness of the deck, the shouts of the brigands came up. They were stumbling about. But the ramming of our trap went on, and I saw that it was beginning to yield.

"We've got to go, Anita!"

From out of the darkness which hung like a shroud over the deck an occasional flash came up, unaimed, wide of our windows. But the darkness was dissipating. I could see now the dim glow of the deck lights, blurred as through a heavy fog.

I dropped another of the bombs.

"Put on your helmet."

"Yes - yes, I will. You put yours on."

We had them adjusted in a moment. Our Erentz motors were pumping.

I gripped her. "Put out your helmet light."

She extinguished it. I handed her my projector.

"Hold it a moment. I'm going to take that belt of bombs."

The trap door was all but broken under the ramming blows of the men. I leaped over the body of the dead duty man, seized the belt of bombs and strapped it around my waist.

"Give me the projector."

She handed it to me. The trap door burst upward! A man's head and shoulders appeared. I fired a bullet into him - the leaden pellet singing down through the yellow powder flash that spat from the projector's muzzle.

The brigand screamed, and dropped back out of sight. There was confusion at the ladder top. I flung a bomb at the broken trap. A tiny heat ray came wavering up through the opening, but went wide of us.

The instrument room was in darkness. I clung to Anita.

"Hold on to my hand. You go first - here is the ladder!"

We found it in the blackness, mounted it and went through the cubby's roof-trap.

I took another look and dropped another bomb beside us. The four foot space up here between the cubby roof and the overhead dome, went black. We were momentarily concealed.

Anita located the manual levers of the lock-entrance.

"Here, Gregg."

I shoved at them. Fear leaped in me that they would not operate. But they swung. The tiny port opened wide to receive us. We clambered into the small air-chamber; the door slid closed, just as a flash from below struck at it. The brigands had seen our cloud of darkness and were firing up through it.

In a moment we were out on the dome top. A sleek, rounded spread of glassite, with broad aluminite girders. There were cross ribs which gave us a footing, and occasionally projections - streamline fin-tips, the casings of the upper rudder shafts, and the upstanding stubby funnels into which helicopters were folded.

We moved along the central footpath and crouched by a six-foot casing. The stars and the glowing Earth were over us. The curving dome top - a hundred feet or so in length, and bulging thirty feet wide beneath us - glistened in the Earthlight. It was a sheer drop and down these curving sides past the ship's hull, a hundred feet to the rocks on which the vessel rested. The towering wall of Archimedes was beside us; and beyond the brink of the ledge the thousands of feet down to the plains.

I saw the lights of Miko's band down there. He had stopped signaling. His little lights were spread out, bobbing as he and his men advanced up the crater's foothills, coming to join the ship.

I had an instant's glimpse. Anita and I could not stay here. The brigands would follow us up in a moment. I saw no exterior ladder. We would have to take our chances and jump.

There were brigands down there on the rocks. I saw three or four helmeted figures, and they saw us! A bullet whizzed by us, and then came the flash of a hand ray.

I touched Anita. "Can you make the leap? Anita dear...."

Again it seemed that this must be farewell.

"Gregg, dear one, we've got to do it!"

Those waiting figures would pounce on us.

"Anita, lie here a moment."

I jumped up and ran twenty feet toward the bow; then back toward the stern, flinging down the last of my bombs. The darkness was like a cloud down there, enveloping the outer brigands. But up there we were above it, etched by the starlight and Earthglow.

I came back to Anita. "We'll have to chance it now."

"Gregg...."

"Good-bye, dear. I'll jump first, down this side, you follow."

To leap into that black patch, with the rocks under it....

"Gregg -"

She was trying to tell me to look overhead. She gestured, "Gregg, see!"

I saw it, out over the plains, a little speck amid the stars. A moving speck, coming toward us!

"Gregg, what is it?"

I gazed, held my breath. A moving speck out there. A blob now. And then I realized it was not a large object, far away, but small, and already very close - only a few hundred feet off, dropping toward the top of our dome. A narrow, flat, ten foot object, like a wingless volplane. There were no lights on it, but in the Earthlight I could see two crouching, helmeted figures riding it.

"Anita! Don't you remember!"

I was swept with dawning comprehension. Back in the Grantline camp Snap and I had discussed how to use the *Planetara's* gravity plates. We had gone to the wreck and secured them, had rigged this little volplane flyer....

The brigands on the rocks saw it now. A flash went up at it. One of the figures crouching on it opened a flexible fabric like a wing over its side. I saw another flash from below, harmlessly striking the insulated shield.

I gasped to Anita, "Light your helmet! It's from Grantline! Let them see us!"

I stood erect. The little flying platform went over us, fifty feet up, circling, dropping to the dome top.

I waved my helmet light. The exit lock from below - up which we had come - was near us. The advancing brigands were already in it! I had forgotten to demolish the manuals. And I saw that the darkness down on the rocks was almost gone now, dissipating in the airless night. The brigands down there began firing up at us.

It was a confusion of flashing lights. I clutched at Anita.

"Come this way - run!"

The platform barely missed our heads. It sailed lengthwise of the dome top, and crashed silently on the central runway near the stern tip. Anita and I ran to it.

The two helmeted figures seized us, shoved us prone on the metal platform. It was barely four feet wide; a low railing, handles with which to cling, and a tiny hooded cubby in front.

"Gregg!"

"You, Snap!"

It was Snap and Venza. She seized Anita, held her crouching in place. Snap flung himself face down at the controls.

The brigands were out on the dome now. I took a last shot as we lifted. My bullet punctured one of them: he slid, fell scrambling off the rounded dome and dropped out of sight.

Light rays and silent flashes seemed to envelope us. Venza held the side shields higher.

We tilted, swayed crazily, and then steadied.

The ship's dome dropped away beneath us. The rocks of the

open ledge were beneath us. Then the abyss, with the moving, climbing specks of Miko's lights far down.

I saw, over the side shield, the already distant brigand ship resting on the ledge with the massive Archimedes' wall behind it. A confusion back there of futile flashing rays.

It all faded into a remote glow as we sailed smoothly up into the starlight and away, heading for the Grantline camp.

XXXIII

"Wake up. Gregg! They're coming!"

I forced myself to consciousness. "Coming -"

I leaped from my bunk, followed Snap with a rush into the corridor.

We had returned safely to the Grantline camp. Anita and I found ourselves exhausted from lack of sleep, our arduous climb of Archimedes and that tense time on the brigand ship. On the flight back, Snap had explained how the landing of the ship on Archimedes was observed through the Grantline telescope. They had read with amazement my signals to the brigands. Snap had rushed to completion the first of our flying platforms. Then he had seen Miko's signals from the crater base, seen the lights and the fight to capture Anita and me, and had come to rescue us.

Back at the camp we were given food, and Grantline forced me to try to sleep.

"They'll be on us in a few hours, Gregg. Miko wall have joined them by now. He'll lead them to us. You must rest, for we need everyone at his best."

And surprisingly, in the midst of the camp's turmoil of last minute activities, I slept soundly until Snap called me, telling me the ship was coming.

The corridor echoed with the tramp of Grantline's busy crew. But there was no confusion; a grim calmness had settled on everyone.

Anita and Venza rushed up to join us. "It's in sight!"

There was no need of going to the instrument room. From the windows fronting the brink of the cliff the brigand ship was plainly visible. It came sailing from Archimedes, a dark shape blurring the stars. All its lights were extinguished save a single white search beam in the bow peak, slanting diagonally down.

The beam presently caught our group of buildings; its glare shone in the windows as it clung for a moment. I could envisage the triumphant curiosity of Potan and his men up there, gazing along the beam.

We had dimmed the lights to conserve our power, and to enable the Erentz motors to run at full capacity. Our buildings would have to withstand the brigands' rays which soon would be upon us.

Outside on our dim, Earthlit cliff, the tiny lights showed where our few guards were lurking. As I stood at the window watching the incoming ship, Grantline's voice sounded:

"Call in those men! Ring the call-lights, Franck!"

The siren buzzed over the camp's interior; the warning call-lights on the roof brought in the outer guards. They came running to the admission ports, which had been repaired after Miko disabled them.

The guards came in. We dimmed our lights further. The treasure sheds were black against the cliff behind us. No need for guards there - we reasoned the brigands would not attempt to move it until our buildings were captured. But, if they should try it, we were prepared to defend it.

In the dim light we crouched. A silence was upon us save for the clanging in the workshop down the corridor. Most of us wore our Erentz suits, with helmets ready, though I am sure there was not a man of us but who prayed he might not have to go out. At many of the windows - our weakest points to withstand the rays - insulated fabric sheets were hung like curtains.

The brigand ship slowly advanced. It was soon over the opposite rim of our little crater. Its searchbeam swung about the rim and down the valley.

My thoughts ran like a turgid stream as I stood tensely watching.

Four hours ago I had sent that flash signal to Earth. If it was received, a patrol ship could come to our rescue and arrive here in another eight hours - or perhaps even less.

Ah, that "if!" *If* the signal was received! *If* the patrol ship were immediately available. *If* it started at once....

Eight hours at the very least. I tried to assure myself that we could hold out that long.

The brigand ship crossed the opposite crater rim. It dropped lower. It seemed poised over the crater valley, almost at our own level and less than two miles from us. Its searchbeam vanished. For a moment it hung, a sleek, cylindrical silver shape, gleaming in the Earthlight.

Snap looked at me and murmured, "It's descending."

It slowly settled, cautiously picked its landing place amid the crags and pits of the tumbled, scarred valley floor. It came to rest, a vague, menacing silver shape lurking in the lower shadows, close at the foot of the inner opposite crater wall.

A few moments of tense waiting passed. Soon tiny lights were moving down there, some out on the rocks near the ship, others up under its deck dome.

A stab of searchlight shot across the valley, swung along our ledge and clung with its glaring ten foot circle to the front of our main building. Then a ray flashed.

The assault had begun!

XXXIV

It seemed, with that first shot from the enemy, that a great relief came to us - an apprehension fallen away. We had anticipated this moment for so long, dreaded it. I think all our men felt it. A shout went up:

"Harmless!"

It was not that. But our building withstood it better than I had feared. It was a flash from a large electronic projector mounted on the deck of the brigand ship. It stabbed up from the shadows across the valley at the foot of the opposite crater wall, a beam of vaguely fluorescent light. Simultaneously the search-light vanished.

The stream of electrons caught the front face of our main building in a six foot circle. It held a few seconds, vanished, then stabbed again, and still again. Three bolts. A total, I suppose, of nine or ten seconds.

I was standing with Grantline at a front window. We had rigged an oblong of insulated fabric like a curtain; we stood peering, holding the curtain cautiously aside. The ray struck some twenty feet away from us.

"Harmless!" The men shouted it with derision.

But Grantline swung on them: "Don't get that idea!"

An interior signal panel was beside Grantline. He called the duty men in the instrument room.

"It's over. What are your readings?"

The bombarding electrons had passed through the outer shell of the building's double wall, and been absorbed in the rarefied, magnetized aircurrent of the Erentz circulation. Like poison in a man's veins, reaching his heart, the free alien electrons had disturbed the motors. They accelerated, then retarded. Pulsed unevenly, and drew added power from the reserve tanks. But they had normalized at once when the shot was past. The duty man's voice sounded from the grid in answer to Grantline's question:

"Five degrees colder in your building. Can't you feel it?"

The disturbed, weakened Erentz system had allowed the outer cold to radiate through a trifle. The walls had had a trifle extra explosive pressure from the air. A strain - but that was all.

"It's probably their most powerful single weapon, Gregg," said Grantline.

I nodded, "Yes, I think so."

I had smashed the real giant, with its ten mile range. The ship was only two miles from us, but it seemed as though this projector were exerted to its distance limit. I had noticed on the deck only one of this type. The others, paralyzing rays and heat rays, were less deadly.

Grantline commented: "We can withstand a lot of that bombardment. If we stay inside -"

That ray, striking a man outside, would penetrate his Erentz suit within a few seconds, we could not doubt. We had, however, no intention of going out unless for dire necessity.

"Even so," said Grantline, "a hand shield would hold it off for a certain length of time."

We had an opportunity a moment later to test our insulated shields. The bolt came again. It darted along the front face of the building, caught our window, and clung. The double window shelves were our weakest points. The sheet of flashing Erentz current was transparent; we could see through it as though it were glass. It moved faster, but was thinner at the windows than the walls. We feared the bombarding electrons might cross it, penetrate the inner shell and, like a lightning bolt, enter the room.

We dropped the curtain corner. The radiance of the bolt was dimly visible. A few seconds, then it vanished again, and behind the shield we had not felt a tingle.

"Harmless!"

But our power had been drained nearly an aeron, to neutralize the shock to the Erentz current. Grantline said:

"If they kept that up, it would be a question of whose power supply would last longer. And it would not be ours.... You saw our lights fade when the bolt was striking?"

But the brigands did not know we were short of power. And to fire the projector with a continuous bolt would, in thirty minutes, perhaps, have exhausted their own power reserve.

"I won't answer them," Grantline declared. "Our game is to sit defensive. Conserve everything. Let them make the leading moves."

We waited half an hour; but no other shot came. The valley floor was patched with Earthlight and shadow. We could see the vague outline of the brigand ship backed up at the foot of the opposite crater wall. The form of its dome over the illuminated deck was visible, and the line of its tiny hull ovals.

On the rocks near the ship, helmet lights of prowling brigands occasionally showed.

Whatever activity was going on down there we could not see with the naked eye. Grantline did not use our telescope at first. To connect it, even for local range, drew on our precious ammunition of power. Some of the men urged that we search the sky with the telescope. Was our rescue ship from Earth coming? But Grantline refused. We were in no trouble yet. And every delay was to our advantage.

"Commander, where shall I put these helmets?"

A man came wheeling a pile of helmets on a small truck.

"At the manual port - in the other building."

Our weapons and outside equipment were massed at the main exit locks of the large building. But we might want to go out through smaller locks too. Grantline sent helmets there; suits were not needed, as most of us were garbed in them now.

Snap was still in the workshop. I went there during this first half-hour of the attack. Ten of our men were busy there with the little flying platforms and the fabric shields.

"How goes it, Snap?"

"Almost all ready."

He had six of the platforms, including the one we had already used, and more than a dozen hand shields. At a squeeze, all of us could ride on these six little vehicles. We might *have* to ride them! We planned that, in event of disaster to the buildings, we could at least escape in this fashion. Food supplies and water were now being placed at the ports.

Depressing preparations! Our buildings uninhabitable, a rush out and away, abandoning the treasure.... Grantline had never mentioned such a contingency, but I noticed, nevertheless, that preparations were being made.

Snap's voice was raised over the clang of the workmen bolting the gravity plates of the last platform:

"Only that one projector, Gregg?"

"They gave us four blasts; but just the one projector. Their strongest."

He grinned. He wore no Erentz suit as yet. He stood in torn grimy work trousers and a bedraggled shirt, with the inevitable red eyeshade holding back his unruly hair. Around his waist was the weighted belt, and there were weights on his shoes for gravity stability.

"Didn't hurt us much."

"No."

"When I get the tube panels in this thing I'll be finished. It'll take another half-hour. Then I'll join you. Where are you stationed?"

I shrugged. "I was at a front window with Johnny. Nothing to do as yet."

Snap went back to his work. "Well, the longer they delay, the better for us. If only your signal got through, Gregg, we'll have a rescue ship here in a few hours more!"

Ah, that *if!*

I turned away. "Can't help you, Snap?"

"No.... Take those shields," he added to one of the men.

"Take them where?"

"To Grantline. He'll tell you where to put them."

The shields were wheeled away on a little cart. I followed it. Grantline sent it to the back exit.

"No other move from them yet, Johnny?"

"No. All quiet."

"Snap's almost finished."

The brigands presently made another play. A giant heat-ray beam came across the valley. It clung to our front wall for nearly a minute.

Grantline got the report from the instrument room. He laughed.

"That helped rather than hurt us. Heated the outer wall. Franck took advantage of it and eased up the motors."

We wondered if Miko knew that. Doubtless he did, for the heat-ray was not used again.

Then came a zed-ray. I stood at the window, watching it, faint sheen of beam in the dimness; it crept with sinister deliberation along our front wall, clung momentarily to our shielded windows, and pried with its revealing glow into Snap's workshop.

"Looking us over," Grantline commented. "I hope they like what they see."

I knew that he did not feel the bravado that was in his tone. We had nothing but small hand weapons: heat-rays, electronic projectors, and bullet projectors. All for very short range fighting. If Miko had not known that before, he could at least make a good guess at it after the careful zed-ray inspection. With his ship down there two miles away, we were powerless to reach him. It seemed that Miko was now testing all his mechanisms. A light flare went up from the dome peak of the ship. It rose in a slow arc over the valley, and burst. For a few seconds the two mile circle of crags was brilliantly illumined. I stared, but I had to shield my eyes against the dazzling actinic glare, and I could see nothing. Was Miko making a zed-ray photograph of our interiors? We had no way of knowing.

He was testing his short range projectors now. With my eyes again accustomed to the normal Earthlight in the valley, I could see the stabs of electronic beams, the Martian paralyzing rays and heat beams. They darted out like flashing swords from the rocks near the ship.

Then the whole ship and the crater wall behind it seemed to shift sidewise as a Benson curve light spread its glow about the ship, with a projector curve beam coming up and touching the window through which I was peering.

"Haljan, come look at these damn girls! Commander - shall I stop them? They'll kill themselves, or kill us - or smash something!"

We followed the man into the building's broad central corridor. Anita and Venza were riding a midget platform! Anita, in her boyish black garb; Venza, with a flowing white Venus-robe. They lay on the tiny six foot long oblong of metal, one manipulating its side shields, the other at the controls. As we arrived, the platform came sliding down the narrow confines of the corridor, lurching, barely missing a door projection. Up to the low vaulted ceiling, then down to the floor.

It sailed over our heads, rising over us as we ducked. Anita waved her hand.

Grantline gasped, "By the infernal!"

I shouted, "Anita, stop!"

But they only waved at us, skimming down the length of the corridor, seeming to avoid a smash a dozen times by the smallest margin of chance, stopping miraculously at the further end, hanging poised in mid-air, wheeling, coming back, undulating up and down.

Grantline clung to me. "By the gods of the airways!"

In spite of my astonished horror, I could not but share Grantline's admiration. Three or four other men were watching. The girls were amazingly skillful, no doubt of that. There was not a man among us who could have handled that gravity platform indoors, not one who would have had the brash temerity to try it.

The platform landed with the grace of a humming bird at our feet, the girls dexterously balancing so that it came to rest swiftly, without the least bump.

I confronted them. "Anita, what are you doing?"

She stood up, flushed and smiling. "Practicing."

"What for?"

Venza's roguish eyes twinkled at me. Her hands went to her slim hips with a gesture of defiance.

She asked, "Are you speaking for yourself or the Commander?"

I ignored her. "What for?"

"Because we're good at it," Anita retorted. "Better than any of you men. If you should need us, we're ready...."

"We won't!" I said shortly.

"But if you should...."

Venza put in, "If Snap and I hadn't come for you, you wouldn't be here, Gregg Haljan. I didn't notice you were so horrified to see me holding that shield up over you!"

It silenced me.

She added, "Commander, let us alone. We won't smash anything."

Grantline laughed. "I hope you won't!"

A warning call took us back to the front window. The brigands' searchlight was again being used. It swept slowly along the length of the cliff. Its circle went down the cliff steps to the valley floor, and came sweeping up again. Then it went up to the observatory platform at the summit above us, then over to the ore sheds.

We had no men outside, if that was what the brigands wanted to determine. The searchbeam presently vanished. It was replaced immediately by a zed-ray, which darted at once to our treasure sheds and clung.

That stung Grantline into his first action. We flung our own zed-ray down across the valley. It reached the brigand ship and the blurred interior of the cabins.

"Try the searchbeam, Franck."

The zed-ray went off. We gazed down our searchlight which clung to the dome of the distant enemy vessel. We could see movement there.

"The telescope," Grantline ordered.

The dynamos hummed. The telescope finder glowed and clarified. On the deck of the ship we saw the brigands working with the assembling of tiny ore carts. A deck landing port was open. The ore carts were being carried out through a port lock and down a landing incline. And on the rock outside, we saw several of the carts, tiny rail sections and the section of an ore chute.

Miko was unloading his mining apparatus! He was making ready to come up for the treasure!

The discovery, startling as it was, nevertheless, was far overshadowed by an imperative danger alarm from our main building. Brigands were outside on our ledge! Miko's search-beam, sweeping the ledge a moment before, had carefully avoided revealing them. It had been done just for that purpose, no doubt - to make us feel sure the ledge was unoccupied and thus to guard against our own light making the search.

But there was a brigand group close outside our walls! By the merest chance the radiating glow from our searchray had shown the helmeted figures scurrying for shelter.

Grantline leaped to his feet.

We rushed from the rear port exit which was nearest us. The giant bloated figures had been seen running along the outside of the connecting corridor, in this direction. But before we ever got there, a new alarm came. A brigand was crouching at a front corner of the main building!

His hydrogen heat torch had already opened a rift in the wall!

XXXV

"In with you!" ordered Grantline. "Get your helmets on! How many? Six. Enough - get back there, Williams - you were last. The lock won't hold any more."

I was one of the six who jammed into the manual exit lock. We went through it; in a moment we were outside. It was less than three minutes since the prowling brigand had been seen.

Grantline touched me just as we emerged. "Don't wait for orders? Get him."

"That fellow with the torch -"

"Yes. I'm with you."

We went out with a rush. We had already discarded our shoe and belt weights. I leaped, regardless of my companions.

The scurrying Martians had disappeared. Through my visor bull's-eye I could see only the Earthlit rocky surface of the ledge. Beside me stretched the dark wall of our building.

I bounded toward the front. The brigand with the torch had been at the front corner. I could not see him from here; he had been crouching just around the angle.

I had a tiny bullet projector, the best weapon for short range outdoors. I was aware of Grantline close behind me.

It took only a few of my giant leaps. I handed at the corner, recovered my balance and whirled around to the front.

The Martian was here, a giant misshapen lump as he crouched. His torch was a little stab of blue in the deep shadow enveloping him. Intent upon his work, he did not see me. Perhaps he thought his fellow men had broken our exits by now.

I landed like a leopard upon his back and fired, my weapon muzzle ramming him. His torch fell hissing with a silent rain of blue fire upon the rocks.

As my grip upon him made audiphone contact, his agonized scream rattled the diaphragms of my ear grids with horrible, deafening intensity.

He lay writhing under me; then was still. His scream choked into silence. His suit deflated within my encircling grip. He was dead: my leaden, steel-tipped pellet had punctured the double surface of his Erentz fabric; penetrated his chest.

Grantline had leaped, landing beside me. "Dead?"

"Yes."

I climbed from the inert body. The torch had hissed itself out. Grantline swung to our building corner, and I leaned down with him to examine it. The torch had fused and scarred the wall, burned almost through. A pressure rift had opened. We could see it, a curving gash in the metal wall-plate like a crack in a glass window pane.

I went cold. This was serious damage. The rarefied Erentz air would seep out. It was leaking now: we could see the magnetic radiance of it all up the length of the ten foot crack. The leak would change the pressure of the Erentz system, constantly lower it, demanding steady renewal. The Erentz motors would overheat; some might go bad from the strain.

Grantline stood gripping me. "Damn bad."

"Yes. Can't we repair it, Johnny?"

"No. Would have to take that whole plaster section out, shut off the Erentz plant and exhaust the interior air of all this bulkhead. Day's job - maybe more."

And the crack would get worse, I knew. It would gradually spread and widen. The Erentz circulation would fail. All our power would be drained struggling to maintain it. This brigand who had unwittingly committed suicide by his daring act had accomplished more than he had perhaps realized. I could envisage our weapons, useless from the lack of power. The air in our buildings turned fetid and frigid; ourselves forced to the helmets. A rush out to abandon the camp and escape. The building exploding, scattering into a litter on the ledge like a child's broken toy. The treasure abandoned, with the brigands coming up and loading it on their ship.

Our defeat. In a few hours now - or minutes. This crack could slowly widen, or it could break suddenly at any time. Disaster, come now so abruptly upon us at the very start of the brigand attack....

Grantline's voice in my audiphone broke my despairing thoughts.

"Bad. Come on, Gregg. Nothing to do here."

We were aware that our other four men had run along the building's other side. They emerged now - with the running brigands in front of them, rushing out toward the stairs on the ledge. Three giant Martian figures in flight, with our four men chasing.

A brigand fell to the rocks by the brink of the ledge. The others reached the descending staircase, tumbled down it with reckless leaps.

Our men turned back. Before we could join them, the enemy ship down in the valley sent up a cautious searchbeam which located its returning men. Then the beam swung up to the ledge, landing upon us.

We stood confused, blinded by the brilliant glare. Grantline stumbled against me.

"Run, Gregg! They'll be firing at us."

We dashed away. Our companions joined us, rushing back for the port. I saw it open, reinforcements coming out to help us - half a dozen figures carrying a ten foot insulated shield. They could barely get it through the port.

The Martian searchray vanished. Then almost instantly the electronic ray came with its deadly stab. Missed us at first, as we ran for the shield, carrying it back to the port, hiding behind it.

The ray stabbed once or twice more.

Whether Miko's instruments showed him how badly damaged our front wall was, we never knew. But I think that he realized. His searchbeam clung to it, and his zed-ray pried into our interiors.

The brigand ship was active now. We were desperate; we used our telescope freely for observation. Miko's ore carts and mining apparatus were unloaded on the rocks. The rail sections were being carried a mile out, nearly to the center of the valley. A subsidiary camp was being established there, only a mile from the base of our cliff, but still far beyond reach of our weapons. We could see the brigand lights down there.

Then the ore chute sections were brought over. We could see Miko's men carrying some of the giant projectors, mounting them in the new position. Power tanks and cables. Light flare catapults - small mechanical cannons for throwing illuminating bombs.

The enemy searchlight constantly raked our vicinity. Occasionally the giant electronic projector flung out its bolt as though warning us not to dare leave our buildings.

Half an hour went by. Our situation was even worse than Miko could know. The Erentz motors were running hot - our power draining, the crack widening. When it would break, we could not tell; but the danger was like a sword over us.

An anxious thirty minutes for us, this second interlude. Grantline called a meeting of all our little force, with every man having his say. Inactivity was no longer a feasible policy. We recklessly used our power to search the sky. Our rescue ship might be up there; but we could not see it with our now disabled instruments. No signals came. We could not - or, at least, did not - receive them.

"They wouldn't signal," Grantline protested. "They'd know the Martians would be more likely to get the signal than us. Of what use to warn Miko?"

But he did not dare wait for a rescue ship that might or might not be coming! Miko was playing the waiting game now - making ready for a quick loading of the ore when we were forced to abandon our buildings.

The brigand ship suddenly moved its position! It rose up in a low flat arc, came forward and settled in the center of the valley where the carts and rail sections were piled, and the outside projectors newly mounted on the rocks.

The brigands now began laying the rails from the ship toward the base of our cliff. The chute would bring the ore down from the ledge, and the carts would take it to the ship. The laying of the rails was done under cover of occasional stabs from the electronic projector.

And then we discovered that Miko had made still another move. The brigand rays, fired from the depth of the valley, could strike our front building, but could not reach all our ledge. And from the ship's newer and nearer position this disadvantage to us was intensified. Then abruptly we realized that under cover of darkness bombs, an electronic projector and searchray had been carried to the top of the crater rim, diagonally across and only half a mile from us. Their beams shot down, raking all our vicinity from this new angle.

I was on the little flying platform which sallied out as a test to attack these isolated projectors. Snap and I, and one other volunteer, went. He and I held the shield; Snap handled the controls.

Our exit port was on the lee side of the building from the hostile searchbeam. We got out unobserved and sailed upward; but soon a light from the ship caught us. And the projector bolts came up....

Our sortie only lasted a few minutes. To me, it was a confusion of crossing beams, with the stars overhead, the swaying little platform under me, and the shield tingling in my hands when the blasts struck us. Moments of blurred terror....

The voice of the man beside me sounded in my ears: "Now, Haljan, give them one!"

We were up over the peak of the rim with the hostile projectors under us. I gauged our movement, and dropped an explosive powder bomb.

It missed. It flared with a puff on the rocks, twenty feet from where the two projectors were mounted. I saw that two helmeted figures were down there. They tried to swing their grids upward, but could not get them vertical to reach us. The ship was firing at us, but it was far away. And Grantline's searchbeam was going full power, clinging to the ship to dazzle them.

Snap circled them. As we came back I dropped another bomb. Its silent puff seemed littered with flying fragments of the two projectors and the bodies of the men.

We swiftly flew back to our base.

It decided Grantline. For an hour past Snap and I had been urging our plan to use the gravity platforms. To remain inactive was sure defeat now. Even if our buildings did not explode - if we thought to huddle in them, helmeted in the failing air - then Miko could readily ignore us and proceed with his loading of the treasure under our helpless gaze. He could do that now with safety - if we refused to accept the challenge - for we could not fire through the windows and must go out to meet this threat.

To remain defensive would end inevitably in our defeat. We all knew it now. The waiting game was Miko's - not ours.

The success of our attack upon the distant isolated projectors, heartened us. Yet it was a desperate offensive upon which we decided!

We prepared our little expedition at the larger of the exit ports. Miko's zed-ray was watching all our interior movements. We made a brave show of activity in our workshop with abandoned ore carts which were stored there. We got them out, started to recondition them.

It seemed to fool Miko. His zed-ray clung to the workshop, watching us. And at the distant port we gathered the platforms, shields, helmets, bombs, and a few hand projectors.

There were six platforms - three of us upon each. It left four people to remain indoors.

I need not describe the emotion with which Snap and I listened to Venza and Anita pleading to be allowed to accompany us. They urged it upon Grantline, and we took no part. It was too important a decision. The treasure - the life or death of all these men - hung now upon the fate of our venture. Snap and I could not intrude our personal feelings.

And the girls won. Both were undeniably more skillful at handling the midget platforms than any of us men. Two of the six platforms could be guided by them. That was a third of our little force! And of what use to go out and be defeated, leaving the girls here to meet death almost immediately afterward?

We gathered at the port. A last minute change made Grantline order six of his men to remain to guard the buildings. The instruments, the Erentz system, all the appliances had to be attended.

It left four platforms, each with three men - Grantline at the controls of one of them. And upon two of the others, Venza rode with Snap and I with Anita.

We crouched in the shadows outside the port. So small an army, sallying out to bomb this enemy vessel or be killed in the attempt! Only sixteen of us. And thirty or so brigands well armed.

I envisioned then this tiny Moon crater, the scene of this battle we were waging. Struggling humans, desperately trying to kill!

Anita drew me down on the platform. "Ready, Gregg."

The others were rising. We lifted, moved slowly out and away from the protective shadows of the building.

XXXVI

Grantline led us. We held about level. Five hundred feet beneath us the brigand ship lay, cradled on the rocks. When it was still a mile away from us I could see all its outline fairly clearly in the dimness. Its tiny hull windows were dark; but the blurred shape of the hull was visible, and above it the rounded cap of dome, with a dim radiance beneath it.

We followed Grantline's platform. It was rising, drawing the others after it like a tail. I touched Anita where she lay beside me with her head half in the small hooded control bank.

"Going too high."

She nodded, but followed the line nevertheless. It was Grantline's command.

I lay crouched, holding the inner tips of the flexible side shields. The bottom of the platform was covered with the insulated fabric. There were two side shields. They extended upward some two feet, flexible so that I could hold them out to see over them, or draw them up and in to cover us.

They afforded a measure of protection against the hostile rays, though just how much we were not sure. With the platform level, a bolt from beneath could not harm us unless it continued for a considerable time. But the platform, except upon direct flight, was seldom level, for it was a frail, unstable little vehicle! To handle it was more than a question of the controls. We balanced, and helped to guide it with the movement of our bodies - shifting our weight sidewise, or back, or forward to make it dip as the controls altered the gravity pull in its tiny plate sections.

Like a bird, wheeling, soaring, swooping. To me, it was a precarious business.

But now we were in straight flight diagonally upward. The outline of the brigand ship came directly under us. I crouched tense, breathless; every moment it seemed that the brigands must discover us and loose their bolts.

They may have seen us for some moments before they fired. I peered over the side shield down at our mark, then up ahead to get Grantline's firing signal. It seemed long delayed. An added glow down there must have warned Grantline that a shot was coming from there. The tiny red light flared bright on his platform.

I turned on our Benson curve light radiance. We had been dark, but a soft glow now enveloped us. Its sheen went down to the ship to reveal us. But its curving path showed us falsely placed. I saw the little line of platforms ahead of us. They seemed to move suddenly sidewise.

It was everyone for himself now; none of us could tell where the other platforms actually were placed or headed. Anita swooped us sharply down to avoid a possible collision.

"Gregg?"

"Yes. I'm aiming."

I was making ready to drop the small explosive globe bomb. Our search light ray at the camp, answering Grantline's signal, shot down and bathed the enemy ship in a white glare, revealing it for our aim. Simultaneously the brigand bolts came up at us.

I held my bomb out over the shield, calculating the angle to throw it down. The brigand rays flashed around me. They were horribly close; Miko had understood our sudden visible shift and aimed, not where we appeared to be, but approximately where we had been before.

I dropped my bomb hastily at the glowing white ship. The touch of a hostile ray would have exploded it in my hand. I saw others dropping also from our nearby platforms. The explosions from them merged in a confusion of the white glare - and a cloud of black mist as the brigands out on the rocks used their darkness bombs.

We swept past in a blur of leaping hostile beams. Silent battle of lights! Darkness bombs down at the ship struggling to bar our camp searchray. The Benson radiance rays from our passing platforms, curving down to mingle with the confusion. The electronic rays sending up their bolts....

Our platforms dropped some ten dynamitrine bombs in that first passage over the ship. As we sped by, I dimmed the Benson radiance. I peered. We had not hit the ship. Or if we had, the damage was inconclusive. But on the rocks I could see a pile of ore carts scattered - broken wreckage, in which the litter of two or three projectors seemed strewn. And the gruesome deflated forms of several helmeted figures. Others seemed to be running, scattering - hiding in the rocks and pit-holes. Twenty brigands at least were outside the ship. Some were running over toward the base of our camp ledge. The darkness bombs were spreading like a curtain over the valley floor; but it seemed that some of the figures were dragging their projectors away.

We sailed off toward the opposite crater rim. I remember passing over the broken wreckage of Grantline's little spaceship, the *Comet.* Miko's bolts momentarily had vanished. We had hit some of his outside projectors; the others were abandoned, or being dragged to safer positions.

After a mile we wheeled and went back. I suddenly realized that only four platforms were in the re-formed line ahead of us. One was missing! I saw it now, wavering down, close over the ship. A bolt leaped up diagonally from a distant angle on the rocks and caught the disabled platform. It fell, whirling, glowing red - disappeared into the blur of darkness like a bit of heated metal plunged into water.

One out of six of our platforms already lost! Three men of our small force gone!

But Grantline led us desperately back. Anita caught his signal to break our line. The five platforms scattered, dipping and wheeling like frightened birds - blurring shapes, shifting unnaturally in flight as the Benson curve lights were altered.

Anita now took our platform in a long swoop downward. Her tense, murmured voice sounded in my ears:

"Hold off; I'll take us low."

A melee. Passing platform shapes. The darting bolts, crossing like ancient rapiers. Falling blue points of fuse lights as we threw our bombs.

Down in a swoop. Then rising. Away, and then back. This silent warfare of lights! It seemed that around me must be bursting a pandemonium of sound. Yet there was none. Silent, blurred melee, infinitely frightening. A bolt struck us, clung for an instant; but we weathered it. The light was blinding. Through my gloves I could feel the tingle of the over charged shield as it caught and absorbed the hostile bombardment. Under me the platform seemed heated. My little Erentz motors ran with ragged pulse. I got too much oxygen. I was dully smothering....

Then the bolt was gone. I found us soaring upward, horribly tilted. I shifted over.

"Anita! Anita, dear, are you all right?"

"Yes, Gregg. All right."

The melee went on. The brigand ship and all its vicinity were enveloped in dark mist now - a turgid sable curtain, made more dense by the dissipating heavy fumes of our exploding bombs which settled low over the ship and the rocks nearby. The searchlight from our camp strove futilely to penetrate the cloud.

Our platforms were separated. One went by, high over us. I saw another dart close beneath my shield.

"God, Anita!"

"Too close! I didn't see it."

Almost a collision.

"Gregg, haven't we broken the ship's dome yet?"

It seemed not. I had dropped nearly all my bombs. This could not go on much longer. Had it been only about five minutes? Only that? Reason told me so, yet it seemed an eternity of horror.

Another swoop. My last bomb. Anita had brought us into position to fling it. But I could not. A bolt stabbed up from the gloom and caught us. We huddled, pulling the shields up and over us.

Blurred darkness again. Too much to the side now. I had to wait while Anita swung us back. Then we seemed too high.

I waited with my last bomb. The other platforms were occasionally dropping them: I had been too hasty, too prodigal.

Had we broken the ship's dome with a direct hit? It seemed not.

The brigands were sending up catapulted light flares. They came from positions on the rocks outside the ship. They mounted in lazy curves and burst over us. The concealing darkness, broken only by the flares of explosions, enveloped the enemy. Our camp searchlight was still struggling with it. But overhead, where the few little platforms were circling and swooping, the flares gave an almost continuous glare. It was dazzling, blinding. Even through the smoked pane which I adjusted to my visor I could not stand it.

But these were thoughts of comparative dimness. In a patch where the Earthlight struck through the darkness of the rocks, I saw another of our fallen platforms! Snap and Venza?

It was not they, but three figures of our men. One was dead. Two had survived the fall. They stood up, staggering. And in that instant, before the turgid black curtain closed over them, I saw two brigands come rushing. Their hand projectors stabbed at close range. Our men crumpled and fell....

We were in position again. I flung my last missile, watched its light as it dropped. On the dome roof two of Miko's men were crouching. My bomb was truly aimed - perhaps one of the few in all our bombardment which landed directly on the dome roof. But the waiting marksmen fired at it with short range heat projectors and exploded it harmlessly while it was still above them.

We swung up and away. I saw, high above us, Grantline's platform, recognizing its red signal light. There seemed a lull. The enemy fire had died down to only a very occasional bolt. In the confusion of my whirling impressions, I wondered if Miko were in distress. Not that! We had not hit his ship; perhaps we had done little damage indeed! It was we who were in distress. Two of our platforms had fallen - two out of six. Or more, of which I did not know.

I saw one rising off to the side of us. Grantline was over us. Well, we were at least three. And then I saw the fourth.

"Grantline is calling us up, Gregg."

Grantline's signal light was summoning us from the attack. He was a thousand feet or more above us.

I was suddenly shocked with horror. The searchray from our camp suddenly vanished! Anita wheeled us to face the distant ledge. The camp lights showed, and over one of the buildings was a distress light!

Had the crack in our front wall broken, threatening explosion of all the buildings? The wild thought swept me. But it was not that. I could see light stabs from the cliff outside the main building. Miko had dared to send some men to attack our almost deserted camp!

Grantline realized it. His red helmet light semaphored the command to follow him. His platform soared away, heading for the camp, with the other two behind him.

Anita lifted us to follow. But I checked her.

"No! Off to the right, across the valley."

"But Gregg!"

"Do as I say, Anita."

She swung us diagonally away from both the camp and the brigand ship. I prayed that we might not be noticed by the brigands.

"Anita, listen: I've got an idea!"

The attack on the brigand ship was over. It lay enveloped in the darkness of the powder gas cloud and its own darkness bombs. But it was uninjured.

Miko had answered us with our own tactics. He had practically unmanned the ship, no doubt, and had sent his men to our buildings. The fight had shifted. But I was now without ammunition, save for two or three bullet projectors.

Of what use for our platform to rush back? Miko expected that. His attack on the camp was undoubtedly made just for that purpose: to lure us back there.

"Anita, if we can get down on the rocks somewhere near the ship, and creep up unobserved in that blackness...."

I might be able to reach the manual hull lock, rip it open and let the air out. If I could get into its pressure chamber and unseal the inner slide....

"It would wreck the ship, Anita: exhaust all its air. Shall we try it?"

"Whatever you say, Gregg."

We seemed to be unobserved. We skimmed close to the valley floor, a mile from the ship. We headed slowly toward it, sailing low over the rocks.

Then we landed, left the platform. "Let me go first, Anita."

I held a bullet projector. With slow, cautious leaps, we advanced. Anita was behind me. I had wanted to leave her with the platform, but she would not stay. And to be with me seemed at least equally safe.

The rocks were deserted. I thought that there was very little chance that any of the enemy would lurk here. We clambered over the pitted, scarred surface; the higher crags, etched with Earthlight, stood like sentinels in the gloom.

The brigand ship with its surrounding darkness was not far from us. No one was out here. We passed the wreckage of broken projectors, and gruesome, shattered human forms.

We prowled closer. The hull of the ship loomed ahead of us. All dark.

We came at last close against the sleek metal hull side, slid along it to where I was sure the manual lock would be located.

Abruptly I realized that Anita was not behind me! Then I saw her at a little distance, struggling in the grip of a giant helmeted figure! The brigand lifted her - turned, and ran.

I did not dare fire. I bounded after them along the hull-side, around under the curve of the pointed bow, down along the other side.

I had mistaken the hull port location. It was here. The running, bounding figure reached it, slid the panel. I was only fifty feet away - not much more than a single leap. I saw Anita being shoved into the pressure lock. The Martian flung himself after her.

I fired at him in desperation, but missed. I came with a rush. And as I reached the port, it slid closed in my face, barring me!

XXXVII

With puny fists I pounded the panel. A small pane in it was transparent. Within the lock I could see the blurred figures of Anita and her captor - and it seemed, another figure there. The lock was some ten feet square, with a low ceiling. It glowed with a dim tube-light.

I strained at it with futile, silent effort. The mechanism was here to open this manual; but it was now clasped from within so would not operate.

A few seconds, while I stood there in a panic of confusion, raging to get in. This disaster had come so suddenly. I did not plan: I had no thought save to batter my way in and rescue Anita. I recall that I finally beat on the glassite pane with my bullet projector until the weapon was bent and useless. And I flung it with a wild despairing rage at my feet.

They were letting the ship's air-pressure into this lock. Soon they would open the inner panel, step into the secondary chamber - and in a moment more would be within the ship's hull corridor. Anita, lost to me!

The outer panel suddenly opened! I had lunged against it with my shoulder; the giant figure inside slid it. It was taken by surprise! I half fell forward.

Huge arms went around me. The goggled face of the helmet peered into mine.

"So it is you, Haljan! I thought I recognized that little device over your helmet bracket. And here is my little Anita, come back to me again!"

Miko!

This was he. His great bloated arms encircling me, bending me backward, holding me helpless. I saw over his shoulder that Anita was clutched in the grip of another helmeted figure. No giant, but tall for an Earth man - almost as tall as myself. Then the tube light in the room illumined the visor. I saw the face, recognized it. Moa!

I gasped, "So - I've got you - Miko -"

"Got me! You're a fool to the last, Haljan! A fool to the last! But you were always a fool."

I could scarcely move in his grip. My arms were pinned. As he slowly bent me backward, I wound my legs around one of his: it was as unyielding as a steel pillar. He had closed the outer panel; the air pressure in the lock was rising. I could feel it against my suit.

My helmeted head was being forced backward; Miko's left arm held me. In his gloved right hand as it came slowly up over my throat I saw a knife blade, its naked, sharpened metal glistening blue-white in the light from overhead.

I seized his wrist. But my puny strength could not hold him. The knife, against all of my efforts, came slowly down.

A moment of this slow, deadly combat - the end of everything for me.

I was aware of the helmeted figure of Moa casting off Anita - and then the two girls leaping upon Miko. It threw him off his balance, and my hanging weight made him topple forward. He took a step to recover himself; his hand with the knife was flung up with an instinctive, involuntary balancing gesture. And as it came down again, I forced the knife-blade to graze his throat. Its point caught in the fabric of his suit.

His startled oath jangled in my ears. The girls were clawing at him; we were all four scrambling, swaying. With despairing strength I twisted at his wrist. The knife went into his throat. I plunged it deeper.

His suit went flabby. He crumpled over me and fell, knocking me to the floor. His voice, with the horrible gurgling rasp of death in it, rattled my ear-grids.

"Not such a fool - are you, Haljan -"

Moa's helmeted head was close over us. I saw that she had seized the knife, jerked it from her brother's throat. She leaped backward, waving it.

I twisted from beneath Miko's lifeless, inert body. As I got to my feet, Anita flung herself to shield me. Moa was across the lock, back up against the wall. The knife in her hand went up. She stood for the briefest instant regarding Anita and me, holding each other. I thought that she was about to leap upon us. But before I could move, the knife came down and plunged into her breast. She fell forward, her grotesque helmet striking the grid-floor almost at my feet.

"Gregg!"

"She's dead."

"No! She moved! Get her helmet off! There's enough air here."

My helmet pressure indicator was faintly buzzing to show that a safe pressure was in the room. I shut off Moa's Erentz motors, unfastened her helmet and raised it off. We gently turned her body. She lay with closed eyes, her pallid face blue. With our own helmets off, we knelt over her.

"Oh, Gregg - is she dead?"

"No. Not quite - but dying."

"Gregg, I don't want her to die! She was trying to help you there at the last."

She opened her eyes. The film of death was glazing them. But she saw me, recognized me.

"Gregg -"

"Yes, Moa. I'm here."

Her vivid lips were faintly drawn in a smile. "I'm - so glad - you took the helmets off, Gregg. I'm - going - you know."

"No!"

"Going - back to Mars - to rest with the fire-makers - where I came from. I was thinking - maybe you would kiss me, Gregg?"

Anita gently pushed me down. I pressed the white, faintly smiling lips with mine. She sighed, and it ended with a rattle in her throat.

"Thank you - Gregg - closer - I can't talk so loudly -"

One of her gloved hands struggled to touch me, but she had no strength and it fell back. Her words were the faintest of whispers:

"There was no use living - without your love. But I want you to see - now - that a Martian girl can die with a smile -"

Her eyelids fluttered down; it seemed that she sighed and then was not breathing. But on her livid face the faint smile still lingered, to show me how a Martian girl could die.

We had forgotten for the moment where we were. As I glanced up I saw through the inner panel, past the secondary lock, that the hull's corridor was visible. And along its length a group of Martians was advancing! They saw us, and came running.

"Anita! Look! We've got to get out of here!"

The secondary lock was open to the corridor. We jammed on our helmets. The unhelmeted brigands by then were fumbling at the inner panel. I pulled at the lever of the outer panel. The brigands were hurrying, thinking that they could be in time to stop me. One of the more cautious fumbled with a helmet.

"Anita, run! Try and keep your feet."

I slid the outer panel and pushed at Anita. Simultaneously the brigands opened the inner port.

The air came with a tempestuous rush. A blast through the inner port - through the small pressure lock - a wild rush, out to the airless Moon. All the air in the ship madly rushing to escape....

Like feathers, we were blown with it. I recall an impression of the hurtling brigand figures and swift flying rocks under me. A silent crash as I struck.

Then soundless, empty blackness.

XXXVIII

"Is he conscious? We'd better take him back: get his helmet off."

"It's over. We can get back to the camp now. Venza dear, we've won - it's over."

"He hears us!"

"Gregg!"

"He hears us. He'll be all right!"

I opened my eyes, I lay on the rocks. Over my helmet, other helmets were peering, and faint, familiar voices mingled with the roaring in my ears.

"- back to the camp and get his helmet off."

"Are his motors smooth? Keep them right, Snap - he must have good air."

I seemed unhurt. But Anita....

She was here. "Gregg, dear one!"

Anita safe! All four of us here on the Earthlit rocks, close outside the brigand ship.

"Anita!"

She held me, lifted me. I was uninjured. I could stand: I staggered up and stood swaying. The brigand ship, a hundred feet away, loomed dark and silent, a lifeless hulk, already empty of air, drained in the mad blast outward. Like the wreck of the *Planetara* - a dead, useless, pulseless hulk already.

We four stood together, triumphant. The battle was over. The brigands were worsted, almost the last man of them dead or dying. No more than ten or fifteen had been available for that final assault upon the camp buildings. Miko's last strategy. I think perhaps he had intended, with his few remaining men, to take the ship and make away, deserting his fellows.

All on the ship, caught unhelmeted by the explosion, were dead long since.

I stood listening to Snap's triumphant account. It had not been difficult for the flying platforms to hunt down the attacking brigands on the open rocks. We had only lost one more platform.

Human hearts beat sometimes with very selfish emotions. It was a triumphant ending for us, and we hardly gave a thought that half of Grantline's men had perished.

We huddled on Snap's platform. It rose, lurching drunkenly barely carrying us.

As we headed for the Grantline buildings, where still the rift in the wall had not quite broken, there came the final triumph. Miko had been aware of it, and knew he had lost. Grantline's searchlight leaped upward, swept the sky, caught its sought-for object - a huge silver cylinder, bathed brightly in the white searchbeam glare.

The police ship from Earth.

TWO PLANETS CLASH FOR LUNAR TREASURE

Gregg Haljan was aware that there was a certain danger in having the giant spaceship *Planetara* stop off at the moon to pick up Grantline's special cargo of moon ore. For that rare metal - invaluable in keeping Earth's technology running - was the target of many greedy eyes.

But nevertheless he hadn't figured on the special twist the clever Martian brigands would use. So when he found both the ship and himself suddenly in their hands, he knew that there was only one way in which he could hope to save that cargo and his own secret - that would be by turning space-pirate himself and paying the BRIGANDS OF THE MOON back in their own interplanetary coin.

* * * * *

Here is a science-fiction classic, as exciting and ingenious as only a master of super-science could write.

* * * * *

When RAY CUMMINGS took leave of this planet early in 1957, the world of modern science-fiction lost one of its genuine founding fathers. For the imagination of this talented writer supplied a great many of the most basic themes upon which the present superstructure of science-fiction is based. Following the lead of Jules Verne and H. G. Wells, Cummings successfully bridged the gap between the early dawning of science-fiction in the last decades of the Nineteenth Century and the full flowering of the field in these middle decades of the Twentieth.

Born in 1887, Cummings acquired insight into the vast possibilities of future science by a personal association with Thomas Alva Edison. During the 1920's and 1930's, he thrilled millions of readers with his vivid tales of space and time. The infinite and the infinitesimal were all parts of his canvas, and past, present, and future, the interplanetary and the extra-dimensional, all made their initial impact on the reading public through his many stories and novels.

* * * * *

Previously published in an ACE edition is his novel,
The Man Who Mastered Time (D-173).

* * * * *

George Eliot
George Gissing
George MacDonald
George Meredith
George Orwell
George Sylvester Viereck
George Tucker
George W. Cable
George Wharton James
Gertrude Atherton
Gordon Casserly
Grace E. King
Grace Gallatin
Grace Greenwood
Grant Allen
Guillermo A. Sherwell
Gulielma Zollinger
Gustav Flaubert
H. A. Cody
H. B. Irving
H.C. Bailey
H. G. Wells
H. H. Munro
H. Irving Hancock
H. Rider Haggard
H. W. C. Davis
Haldeman Julius
Hall Caine
Hamilton Wright Mabie
Hans Christian Andersen
Harold Avery
Harold McGrath
Harriet Beecher Stowe
Harry Castlemon
Harry Coghill
Harry Houidini
Hayden Carruth
Helent Hunt Jackson
Helen Nicolay
Hendrik Conscience
Hendy David Thoreau
Henri Barbusse
Henrik Ibsen
Henry Adams
Henry Ford
Henry Frost
Henry James
Henry Jones Ford
Henry Seton Merriman
Henry W Longfellow
Herbert A. Giles
Herbert Carter
Herbert N. Casson
Herman Hesse
Hildegard G. Frey
Homer
Honore De Balzac
Horace B. Day
Horace Walpole
Horatio Alger Jr.
Howard Pyle
Howard R. Garis
Hugh Lofting
Hugh Walpole
Humphry Ward
Ian Maclaren
Inez Haynes Gillmore
Irving Bacheller
Isabel Hornibrook
Israel Abrahams
Ivan Turgenev
J.G.Austin
J. Henri Fabre
J. M. Barrie
J. Macdonald Oxley
J. S. Fletcher
J. S. Knowles
J. Storer Clouston
Jack London
Jacob Abbott
James Allen
James Andrews
James Baldwin
James Branch Cabell
James DeMille
James Joyce
James Lane Allen
James Lane Allen
James Oliver Curwood
James Oppenheim
James Otis
James R. Driscoll
Jane Austen
Jane L. Stewart
Janet Aldridge
Jens Peter Jacobsen
Jerome K. Jerome
John Burroughs
John Cournos
John F. Kennedy
John Gay
John Glasworthy
John Habberton
John Joy Bell
John Kendrick Bangs
John Milton
John Philip Sousa
Jonas Lauritz Idemil Lie
Jonathan Swift
Joseph A. Altsheler
Joseph Carey
Joseph Conrad
Joseph E. Badger Jr
Joseph Hergesheimer
Joseph Jacobs
Jules Vernes
Julian Hawthrone
Julie A Lippmann
Justin Huntly McCarthy
Kakuzo Okakura
Kenneth Grahame
Kenneth McGaffey
Kate Langley Bosher
Kate Langley Bosher
Katherine Cecil Thurston
Katherine Stokes
L. A. Abbot
L. T. Meade
L. Frank Baum
Latta Griswold
Laura Dent Crane
Laura Lee Hope
Laurence Housman
Lawrence Beasley
Leo Tolstoy
Leonid Andreyev
Lewis Carroll
Lewis Sperry Chafer
Lilian Bell
Lloyd Osbourne
Louis Hughes
Louis Tracy
Louisa May Alcott
Lucy Fitch Perkins
Lucy Maud Montgomery
Luther Benson
Lydia Miller Middleton
Lyndon Orr
M. Corvus
M. H. Adams
Margaret E. Sangster
Margret Howth
Margaret Vandercook

Margret Penrose
Maria Edgeworth
Maria Thompson Daviess
Mariano Azuela
Marion Polk Angellotti
Mark Overton
Mark Twain
Mary Austin
Mary Catherine Crowley
Mary Cole
Mary Hastings Bradley
Mary Roberts Rinehart
Mary Rowlandson
M. Wollstonecraft Shelley
Maud Lindsay
Max Beerbohm
Myra Kelly
Nathaniel Hawthrone
Nicolo Machiavelli
O. F. Walton
Oscar Wilde
Owen Johnson
P.G. Wodehouse
Paul and Mabel Thorne
Paul G. Tomlinson
Paul Severing
Percy Brebner
Peter B. Kyne
Plato
R. Derby Holmes
R. L. Stevenson
R. S. Ball
Rabindranath Tagore
Rahul Alvares
Ralph Bonehill
Ralph Henry Barbour
Ralph Victor
Ralph Waldo Emmerson
Rene Descartes
Rex Beach
Rex E. Beach
Richard Harding Davis
Richard Jefferies
Richard Le Gallienne
Robert Barr
Robert Frost
Robert Gordon Anderson
Robert L. Drake
Robert Lansing
Robert Lynd
Robert Michael Ballantyne
Robert W. Chambers
Rosa Nouchette Carey
Rudyard Kipling
Samuel B. Allison
Samuel Hopkins Adams
Sarah Bernhardt
Sarah C. Hallowell
Selma Lagerlof
Sherwood Anderson
Sigmund Freud
Standish O'Grady
Stanley Weyman
Stella Benson
Stella M. Francis
Stephen Crane
Stewart Edward White
Stijn Streuvels
Swami Abhedananda
Swami Parmananda
T. S. Ackland
T. S. Arthur
The Princess Der Ling
Thomas A. Janvier
Thomas A Kempis
Thomas Anderton
Thomas Bailey Aldrich
Thomas Bulfinch
Thomas De Quincey
Thomas Dixon
Thomas H. Huxley
Thomas Hardy
Thomas More
Thornton W. Burgess
U. S. Grant
Valentine Williams
Various Authors
Vaughan Kester
Victor Appleton
Victoria Cross
Virginia Woolf
Wadsworth Camp
Walter Camp
Walter Scott
Washington Irving
Wilbur Lawton
Wilkie Collins
Willa Cather
Willard F. Baker
William Dean Howells
William le Queux
W. Makepeace Thackeray
William W. Walter
William Shakespeare
Winston Churchill
Yei Theodora Ozaki
Yogi Ramacharaka
Young E. Allison
Zane Grey

www.ingramcontent.com/pod-product-compliance
Lightning Source LLC
LaVergne TN
LVHW091640100826
845152LV00006B/102/J
* 9 7 8 1 4 2 1 8 2 4 0 2 4 *